Wilting Laughter

Three Tamil Poets

R Cheran, VIS Jayapalan
Puthuvai Ratnathurai

edited and translated by
Chelva Kanaganayakam

We acknowledge the support of the Canada Council for the Arts for our publishing program and the Government of Ontario through the Ontario Arts Council.

Cover image: *Grandma's Courtyard-II*, by Thamotharampillai Shanaathanan, mixed media on paper.

Cover design by Karuna/Digi Media Creations.

Library and Archives Canada Cataloguing in Publication

Wilting laughter : three Tamil poets / by R. Cheran, V.I.S. Jayapalan, Puthuvai Ratnathurai ; edited and translated by Chelva Kanaganayakam.

ISBN 978-1-894770-59-0

1. Tamil poetry—Translations into English. 2. Sri Lanka—Poetry. I. Cheran, R II. Jayapalan, V. I. S. III. Ratnathurai, Puthuvai, 1948- IV. Kanaganayakam, Chelva, 1952-

PL4758.65.E5W54 2009 894.8'1117108 C2009-904816-7

Printed in Canada by Coach House Printing

TSAR Publications
P. O. Box 6996, Station A
Toronto, Ontario M5W 1X7
Canada

www.tsarbooks.com

CONTENTS

Introduction
Chelva Kanaganayakam *vii*

R Cheran

My Land 3
The Past 4
To a Sinhalese Girl 5
Not Parallel Worlds 8
Ritual 9
Summer Fields 10
The Second Sunrise 11
Two Mornings and a Late Night 12
Yaman 14
Demonic Eyes 15
Forgetting 17
Death of a Day 18
The Story of a Severed Leg 19
Vimalathasan, My Brother 21
Letters from an Army Camp 23
The Ghost's Song 28
Roaming 29
A Procession of Skeletons 29
Grave Song 33
Closure 34
Ending Pathways 38
The Elder 40
Love Song 41
The Giant Tree in the Rain Forest 44
Nine Days 45

VIS Jayapalan

Gently Flows the River 49
Speaking to the Sun 50
Dawn 52
The Fences in Our Village 53
Forest and City 54
Duality 56
Prayer 57
A Poem in Blood 59
Our Land and a Lovely Spring 60

Marina's Grief 62
Land of the Singing Fish 64
To Grandmother 65
To a Childhood Sinhalese Friend 67
Children of the Soil 68
If Tears Must Be Our Fate 69
Domesticity 72
Goodbye Mother 73
My Story 74
Unknown Pastures 76
Fragrance 79
A Sunny Day 81
Autumn Thoughts 82
Goodbye 85
A Traveller's Song 87
Life's Poem 89

Puthuvai Ratnathurai

December, a Thing of Beauty 95
Beauty Unseen 96
Writing the Remnants of a Dream 96
A Poet's Fearless Death 100
An Elegy for a Teacher 102
The Temple Across the Field 104
Waiting 107
Crescent Moon 108
Those Days Were Beautiful 109
Yearning 112
The Frolicking Clouds 113
Resurgent Dawn and a Restless Poet 114
The Sculptor and the Statue 116
Moving River 117
Silenced, the Temple Bells 118
The Poet, the Wind, and the Flowers 120
On the Third Day After the Festival 121
Fulfilment 123
Grant Me a Wish 124
Three Questions 125
Relationship 126
Beauty and the Sea 127
Bright Even in the Night 128
Our Folks Are Not Ungrateful 129
Where Snow Falls 131

INTRODUCTION

Wilting Laughter showcases the work of three contemporary Tamil poets. For those who are familiar with the current literary scene in Sri Lanka, these poets and the substantial body of work they have produced over three decades need very little by way of introduction. Their work continues to be read and discussed by Tamils all over the world. For readers unfamiliar with Tamil literature in general, this work is best seen as one more addition to a growing body of translations that recreates in English segments of a literary tradition that began more than twenty centuries ago. Among the classical languages of the world, Tamil is unique in that continues to function as a living language and its ancient literature remains accessible and relevant to this day. The narratives of love and war during the early Sangam Period are not vastly different from the lyrics and political poems of contemporary poets. In fact allusions to ancient and medieval Tamil literature abound in contemporary writing, and to the informed reader these connections are an important way of establishing comparisons and continuities. To write in Tamil is to invoke a long and continuous tradition of genre, poetic form, metaphor, and narrative content. The three poets included in this collection self-consciously draw attention to the literary works of the past, thereby signaling their debt to a rich and lively tradition.

We understand the social and political structures of ancient society largely through literary texts. As chroniclers and as agents of change, ancient and medieval poets have retained a special place in social and cultural history. They have been supported by kings and nourished by the people. When countries flourished, or when they were threatened by upheavals and political turmoil, poets have spoken out, and people paid attention. Both written and oral poetry in Tamil have strong associations with music and song, and that too has been a factor in establishing the centrality of poetry to culture. To this day that tradition has remained intact. This collection, then, is a small tributary that joins a great river.[1]

In a remarkably astute essay, the well-known author B Jeyamohan makes the observation that the tradition of revolutionary poetry in Tamil literature comes to an abrupt end with Subramanya Bharathi in South India and then reappears with the work of R Cheran.[2] While Jeyamohan's concern is with the thematic concerns and impulses that are specific to Cheran's poetry, it can be argued that in a general sense the revolutionary and radical impulse of Bharathi reinvents itself in Sri Lanka in the late 1970s, particularly among poets writing in Tamil. Bharathi's impulse to radicalize his poetry came from the struggle against British imperialism.[3] Bharathi recognized the need for and significance of a poetry that appealed directly to the people without compromising its complexity or depth. For the Tamil poets in Sri Lanka, the revolutionary fervor was associated on the other hand with the rise of Tamil nationalism. To say this is not to attempt a homogenous frame for Tamil poetry in Sri Lanka or to imply that we can assign a precise temporal period for the nationalist struggle. Tamil nationalism began long before the 1970s. In fact its birth can be linked to the work of a number of scholars and thinkers during the colonial period. More specifically, it can be argued that the nationalist question became important when the country gained its independence in 1948. The 1970s, however, witnessed a widespread clamor for autonomy and separatism, accompanied by a gradual increase in militancy. A series of events, involving the Sri Lankan government and the major Tamil political parties, led to an impasse in the 1970s, when the Tamil question became a pervasive presence. The next three decades witnessed the rise of ethnic tension to such a degree that it was hardly possible for anyone to remain unaffected at some level. Starting in 1976, the political and the personal began to intersect in ways that were entirely new. Hence it is hardly surprising that regardless of the many differences in stands and perspectives, a common thread for poets was the immediacy of political assertion. Regardless of region or religious affiliation, most poets who wrote in Tamil felt the urgent need to engage with politics. The revolutionary poetics of Bharathi, which had lain dormant for more than half a century, reappeared in Sri Lanka in the 1970s and 1980s. Cheran is clearly an inheritor of the Bharathi tradition, but it might well be equally true that both VIS Jayapalan and Puthuvai Ratnathurai cherished the poetic ideals of Bharathi.

Political engagement did not mean an acceptance of any particular ideology or consensus about future visions. Among the five militant groups that rose to prominence during that decade, there was no easy agreement about the course of Tamil nationalism. The violence among militant groups during this period is a clear reflection of how murky the horizon turned out to be during these troubled times. Regional, religious, and clan differences were but a few of the centrifugal forces that made life among Tamils an increasingly complex affair. Those who sought democratic solutions stood at a remove from those who advocated militancy. But no one could escape politics, although no particular vision was held to be the ideal. The various militant groups shaped, in many ways, the political trajectory of this time, while the poets and writers became the cultural voice of the Tamils.

To make this claim is not simply to assert that historical circumstance necessitated an involvement with politics in Sri Lanka. For many poets, and certainly for Puthuvai , Jayapalan, and Cheran, poetry and revolution were tied together in the broadest possible sense.[4] These poets were, in their very different ways, chroniclers of the time and were the products of an era that needed poets to write about experiences when it was increasingly difficult to separate day-to-day lives from political conflicts, changes, aspirations, and disappointments. Puthuvai is probably the only poet among the three who consistently identified himself explicitly with one political group. Starting in 1985, he became the official bard of the Liberation Tigers of Tamil Eelam (LTTE), although he did write a large number of poems in which his political commitment was either indirect or absent. Jayapalan, for a brief period in the early 80s, supported the vision of People's Liberation Organization of Tamil Eelam (PLOTE), but for the last twenty years he has remained free of any political affiliation. Cheran has chosen not to identify with any political or militant group, retaining the freedom to express his own views. And this is precisely why the three of them, taken together, offer a particularly strong political and cultural history of the time through their poetry. While it is possible to argue that almost all the writers at this time felt the need to draw attention in their works to the political context of their time, these three poets occupied a different niche. They were seen by their readers as adopting an agential role by taking stands on issues, celebrating or critiquing political decisions, chronicling the individual and collective grief of a people caught in the turmoil of political upheaval. Their personal lives and their poetry were intertwined in ways that allowed for mutual reinforcement. Their poetry energized some and offended others, often resulting in situations that were dangerous. All three were displaced, internally or externally, but all three continued to write with conviction and with a strong sense of urgency. They are certainly not the only major poets of this time. But it would be difficult to write the literary history of this era without acknowledging the importance of their contribution to cultural and political history.

The poetics of writing was, during this period, deeply linked with a sensibility that involved the people and responded to their lives in very intimate ways. Poetry was seen as both an expression and an extension of the thought of the people. These three poets did not see the world around them through the same lens. In fact, their political convictions were at times very different. But they spoke to and for the people, and a strong sense of the oral and the performative runs through their work. All three were poets and lyricists in that many of their poems have been set to music. The politics of the time served as a catalyst to cause a surge in poetic invention, and these three poets were part of a general movement that was clearly different from anything seen between their time and the period in the early part of the twentieth century when Bharathi wrote his wonderful poems of political resistance. Bharathi was conscious of the need to alter the poetic diction and form of the previous century and reshape poetry to appeal to the ordinary reader and listener. Puthuvai and Cheran were intimately connected with the performance of poetry for the public. Drawing from music and drama, they created performances in which people in the remotest villages could watch and listen to their poetry and understand that what was being sung and retold was the story of their own lives.

In an era that gave rise to a substantial number of major poets, the choice of Cheran, Jayapalan, and Puthuvai might well seem strange. Admittedly, the choice is personal, based on a deep appreciation of their diverse poetic talent, but hopefully it is not idiosyncratic. All three are men and they are from Jaffna,[5] which does not make them too representative. But there is a rationale for their selection. They have been the most consistent poets in a long list of authors. Only a handful of other poets—M A Nuhman, S Sivasegaram, M Ponnambalam, S Vilvaratnam, and R Murugaiyan—come to mind, who might claim this temporal scope. All three have written steadily for several decades, producing a substantial corpus that reflects the vicissitudes of history and the changes in their own sensibilities. All three have played other roles in their lives, but they are, by conviction, poets. The self-reflexivity of their poetry is in itself a testimony to their deep commitment to it. Two of them are diasporic, and one chose to remain in Sri Lanka, but all three were deeply conscious of the need to struggle with language, to find an idiom that would reflect and refashion the political concerns of the time. Puthuvai and Jayapalan began publishing in the 70s, while Cheran began in the 80s. All of them are deeply aware of the currents that led to the crises of the 80s, and the many changes and challenges faced by people who were forced to endure an unprecedented number of misfortunes. They realized that it was not possible to be a poet at this time without recognizing that poetics and politics went hand in hand. There are. of course, many other dimensions to their poetry. Puthuvai's preoccupation with the sacred, Jayapalan's love for nature, and Cheran's investment in love poetry are all constitutive elements in their corpus. But all these themes intersect with politics.

Strangely enough, we do not encounter much by way of historical analyses of this period. There were several reasons for this. We do have some specialized studies that have preserved academic rigor and balance. Many of the writings, however, reflect stands and biases rather than objective appraisals. The fact is that if one wishes to understand this turbulent period, one has to turn to literature, particularly poetry. The intersections and divergences in the works of the poets allow us to piece together a complex story of political strife. Poets are our historians and our cultural theorists. They needed to speak simply, directly, and passionately. They spoke to the people in print and through performance, thereby insisting on their relevance. And they recognized that poetry needed to be more than posturing. The last three decades may have been very difficult ones for many reasons, but for the burgeoning of literature these were the best of times.

The publication of *Maranothul Valvom* (We Live Amidst Death) in 1985, an anthology of Sri Lankan poetry in Tamil, comprising eighty-five poems, the work of thirty-two poets, marks a turning point in contemporary Tamil poetry.[6] The preface, written by Cheran, provides a rationale for the title and the thematic grouping of the poems. The immediate purpose of the collection was to bring together a body of poetry that reflected the new political reality, the climate of uncertainty and political violence in the country. In some senses, such a collection was almost inevitable, given the escalation of violence, starting in the 1970s but reaching a critical point with the pogrom of 1983. But the collection is also symptomatic of a larger process involving the role and function of literature in a society where, for several decades, literature had been a somewhat specialized activity. Among the observations that Cheran (who wrote the preface) makes, one needs to note in particular that the collection was seen as part of a larger cultural enterprise in which literature and other cultural forms were being embraced by the public as fundamentals of nationalism and ethnic identity. As he puts it, "In our context, poetry is hardly for silent reading or for the sole enjoyment of intellectuals. It must appeal to the common person."[7] Poetry, together with fiction and drama, now had a much more vital role to play, and this collection points to a radical shift in sensibility and in poetic practice. A new vision, a new style, and a new urgency had entered the literary scene.

The shift in perspective becomes all the more apparent when this anthology is juxtaposed with another collection titled *Pathinoru Eelathu Kavignarkal* (Eleven Eelam Poets) edited by M A Nuhman and A Yesurasa, published a year earlier in 1984.[8] In a pre-emptive gesture, the editors of this anthology claim in their preface that it needs to be seen as a personal anthology, one in which many poets may have been excluded, but those included are clearly among the best poets in Sri Lanka, their work spanning five generations. In the process of showcasing eleven poets, the editors offer a trajectory that begins in the 1940s and moves through various phases to the present. Despite their relevance, both the preface and the poems seem so removed from the concerns and thematic preoccupations of *Maranothul Valvom* that one might wonder how they could have been drawn from the same social scene or appeared within a year of each other.[9] While the preface of *Pathinoru Eelathu Kavignarkal* talks about social consciousness, language, ethnicity, caste hierarchy etc. as matters of concern, the dominant impulse is to foreground the range of poetic forms and artistic skill of the eleven poets considered. The collection provides a sampling of five poems from each poet, and the poems give very little indication of the political crisis in the country. Cheran's poems are the only exception. The differences in the approaches of the two anthologies is striking. The appearance of two such volumes within one year of each other also suggests the confluence of the artistic and the political, a feature that becomes increasingly apparent in the two decades following the publication of *Maranothul Valvom*. Rather than rationalize the appearance of these two collections within one year of each other, one might assert that one marked the close of a trend while the other the birth of another.

To make this point is not to claim that in the one year between the two collections something drastic happened in Sri Lanka to change the sensibility of writers. In fact many poets from the first collection reappear in the second. The more plausible explanation would be that by 1985 it had become increasingly clear that the old world had all but disappeared, giving way to new concerns and priorities. Instead of a socially conscious poetry that was "poetic," now we had a kind of poetry that was part of a larger world view in which lives were being altered in entirely unanticipated ways. In the years following the pogrom of 1983, it was also becoming apparent that a certain pattern, always evident in Tamil literary history, was being reenacted in Sri Lankan literature. In moments of upheaval affecting an entire community, literature renews itself and responds to its new role by accommodating and employing the oral and the local. With all its energy and artistic skill, the poetry of the previous few decades held firmly to convention, not only in its poetic forms, but also in the way it accessed social concerns. The poet as witness still stood apart, aware of social oppression no doubt, but still faithful to an idiom that was shaped by convention. Although critics claim that the previous poetry was not homogenous and that there was a distinct dichotomy between those who were traditional and those who were modernist, the fact is that both were writing within a framework that was "literary." It was really in the 80s that the "oral" dimension took centre stage. As the preface to *Maranothul Valvom* makes clear, "this is a significant phase in the history of Tamil culture. The manifestations of this ethos are evident in plays, street performances, songs, folk dances, documentaries, and in poetry. In poetry this impulse reaches new heights" (p.8). The major poets of the 50s and 60s, and they include Mahakavi, Murugaiyan, and Neelavanan, energized Tamil poetry in many ways. Their diction and their poetic form went back to the oral, but the oral still remained within the literary. Whether people listened to or read their poetry, they were conscious of reaching out to a particular segment of the public. They spoke with conviction, but they spoke to the initiated. Also, for various reasons, they kept clear of the political scene. Cheran, Jayapalan and Puthuvai were nourished by these poets, but they located themselves amongst people, not at the margins.

Maranothul Valvom thus marks the beginning of a trend that continues to this day, as poets who live in Sri Lanka and those who are scattered across the diaspora produce a body of poetry that is in some fundamental ways political and oral. The idea of orality implies more than the inclusion of folk idioms or speech patterns in literature. It suggests a mode of writing in which the rhythms and vocabulary of ordinary speech are molded to sound new and unordinary. The poets do not abandon conventional forms. They simply reshape them to make the ordinary look extraordinary. It is this dimension that sets this poetry apart from much that is written in, say, Singapore or Tamil Nadu. Poetic language is ultimately about difference, about reaching for an idiom that lies beyond the ordinary, but embracing the oral also implies that the poets felt the need to identify with the spoken rather than the written. The challenge for critical practice, then, is to move beyond subjective response and the exigencies of the moment to appraise this poetry as literature. If the new poetry marks a new and important phase, it is equally important that its significance be judged beyond its investment in contemporary politics. Caught in the excitement of the moment, many have written poems that hardly go beyond cliché or tendentious posturing. Quite often a banal rhetoric masquerades as poetry. In the works of these three poets, particularly at their best, the reader or listener experiences the shock of seeing the familiar or the ordinary in extraordinary terms. And this is precisely why their poetry continues to remain relevant, even when the events they speak of have become distant memory.

The objective of this collection is to focus on three poets, all of whom began writing around the same period, to demonstrate how their recent poetry marks a certain kind of resurgence, inspired as much by the political scene as by the realities of diaspora.[10] Two of them—Jayapalan and Cheran—are now diasporic poets while the third—Puthuvai—has remained in Sri Lanka. They are, arguably, three major voices, although it is possible to claim that several others are worthy of equal recognition.[11] In fact, one of the striking features of contemporary poetry is the range of its expression. The poetry of women, for instance, particularly those actively involved in political struggle, adds a dimension that is crucial to this period. This introduction, then, is not so much an attempt to create a hierarchy among poets but to offer some thoughts on poetics and contemporary Tamil poetry in Sri Lanka, based on the work of three poets. In their own ways these three poets, when they are inspired by a particular incident or a sequence of events, are capable of spellbinding power. The overarching rationale of this collection is that in all three poets, in the last two decades, the impulse has been, in different ways, to establish continuities with the past while embracing the oral and the local. They give us a narrative of the struggle and trauma which they experienced first-hand and captured imaginatively in their poetry.

At the very outset it must be acknowledged that in ideological terms Puthuvai occupies a different niche from the other two. The two anthologies mentioned at the beginning do not include his poetry—possibly because of his penchant for tendentious work, which shifted in the mid-1980s from a left perspective to one that fully endorsed the ideology of the LTTE. From the mid-1980s he has been seen as the cultural voice of the LTTE, and much of his recent poetry has focused on the role of the LTTE in relation to the political scene in Sri Lanka. His position as the "official" poet of the LTTE has become foregrounded in critical accounts of his work. Even a generally laudatory critic such as K Sivathamby recognizes the importance of ideology in the poetry of Puthuvai. Sivathamby, one might add, is possibly the only critic who has attempted a serious critical study of the poet, placing him against the backdrop of literary history in Sri Lanka. Equally important perhaps is a long interview with Puthuvai by P Ayngaranesan in which the poet talks about his life, his influences, and his poetry.[12]

Puthuvai thus occupies an ambivalent position, praised on the one hand for his fiery political enthusiasm, and intermittently identified as a major poet. He has been acknowledged more readily as a bard and lyricist rather than a poet. The fact that many of his poems have been set to music further places him within a tradition of song rather than poetry. In fact, Puthuvai has written approximately 600 poems that are more readily recognized as songs. The duality between poetry and song is, however, in the context of Tamil literary history, quite arbitrary. The other two poets, Cheran and Jayapalan, have been political, but have not specifically celebrated the ideological position of any movement in their poetry. They were, inevitably, involved with the strong Marxist thinking that shaped the ethos of the 60s and 70s, and they have responded in one form or another to the political scene. In more recent years, both Cheran and Jayapalan have brought into their poetry a diasporic consciousness that is absent in Puthuvai. However, one of the underlying arguments of this introduction is that Puthuvai too needs to be seen as a major poet, not because of, but in spite of his tendentious poetry and political affiliation. In very different ways, these three poets recognized the need for a poetry that would examine what it meant to be human at a time of crisis, using an idiom that was ordinary and poetic at the same time. They are also very different poets by training and by conviction, and this is precisely why together they shed light on their world in significant ways.

Almost four decades ago, in 1970, Puthuvai began his career as a poet with a collection called *Vanam Sivakkirathu*. Even in these early poems there is a distinct sense of conviction that his poetry must serve a social cause. Neither the literary traditions of the past, nor the empty nature romanticism appealed to him. His poetry needed to celebrate the new and the innovative. There is, of course, a paradox in his assertion, since much of his poetry—even then—was indebted to literary tradition. The metrical patterns of his poetry are suggestive of a tradition that is at once his strength and his point of departure. Making the familiar the subject of his poetry while retaining the artifice of poetic form becomes his forte not only in this collection but also his subsequent ones. In fact there is in the early poetry a conscious distancing from ethnic identities as he identifies with the downtrodden and the poor. There is also an implicit irony in the stance since the conventionality of his role as a champion of the marginalized gives way to a poetry that is deeply traditional. What was perhaps seen as revolutionary several decades before in the poetry of, say, Subramanya Bharathi, comes across now as an attitude rather than conviction. Interestingly, he specifically pays tribute to Bharathi in one of his poems, calling him the source of his inspiration. At this stage, in his first three collections (it is interesting that he calls himself a revolutionary poet on the title page of the third collection), the ordinary stills remains outside the reach of an original poetic idiom. This is the poetry of the 70s, a time when the dominant divide in Jaffna society was based on class and caste. Puthuvai's titles are a clear indication that his sympathies lay with the oppressed, but it is only when he moves away from the overtly didactic that he is able to establish a sense of continuity with the past without forsaking his own voice. There is, for example a short poem titled "A Sneeze Does Not Topple a Mountain" which finds a synthesis of convention and originality:

> A sneeze does not topple a mountain, nor does a drizzle make an ocean;
> brother, empty words do not put food on the table;
> like chillies mashed on stone, the bourgeoisie,
> mash them we must, join forces with me.
> (*Iratha Pushpangal*, 27)

Here (at least in the original) the rhyme scheme retains the sense of artifice, the poetic idiom as it were, while the familiarity of the image, together with the tone, establish a sense of poetic difference.

By the time Puthuvai brought out his next collection, thirteen years had passed, and his commitment to left politics had changed to a preoccupation with nationalist politics, and specifically the LTTE. For the next ten years, Puthuvai wrote under two pseudonyms—Viyasan and Malika—and these poems were then published as a collection in 2003, using his own name. These poems are clearly intended to be tendentious, but their strength lies—at least in many of them—in the way in which public events are seen through the private and the personal. Political poems are not necessarily inferior because they are predominantly message-driven. It is difficult to dismiss the poignancy of many poems written during this period.

At this time Puthuvai also published a number of other poems that were later collected in an anthology. It is primarily in this collection, titled *Puvarasm Veliyum Pulinikkunchukalum* (2005), that one sees the full range of Puthuvai as a poet, and the ways in which the ordinariness of life among the Tamils becomes a cause for celebration, where the natural speaking voice shocks the reader into recognizing the poignancy of the familiar. In his own introduction to the volume, Puthuvai speaks of himself in terms that are strikingly ordinary. The commitment now is to being human, to recording the joys, disappointments, failures of those around him. Interestingly, he titles his introduction *Pulunikunchugal*—diminutive birds—rather than the tall fence. And this is no false modesty. His poetry succeeds within this mental frame of looking at the ordinary and transforming it into something rich and revelatory.

Moments that may have gone unnoticed, moments that are so common that they are hardly noticed, now become charged with emotion and sensuous beauty. The empty streets, the sound of a temple bell, people bathing at wells in the morning—all these are suggestive of a way of life that has now become valuable. Even a domestic scene such as the poet's wife waking him in the morning is now imbued with a poignant significance.

> the temple bells,
> the sound of prayer,
> and my wife's beauty
> as she wakes me
> her hair and cloth
> wrapped together,
> all converge.
> December, a thing of beauty.
> (*Puvarasm Veliyum Pulinikkunchukalum*, 48)

There is very little rhetoric, very little posturing; instead, the simple and almost mundane activities of ordinary people become emblems of cultural significance. In a landscape that has very little to offer by way of mountains and rivers, it is the ritual of bathing, plucking flowers, and responding to silence that becomes significant.

Interestingly, the sacred and the religious now reenter his poetry without all the polemics or the exoticism that one saw in the decades that preceded the 80s. Temples are no longer symbols of social hierarchy and discrimination, although there are several poems that are deeply satirical. For the most part, they become focal points of social cohesiveness. The meticulous care lavished on descriptions of the sacred is partly a result of the author's own background as a sculptor of temple chariots. But the descriptions have a function in that they move beyond sectarian divisions to appeal to a common consciousness. At a time of fragmentation and dispersal, the temple remains a constant, and rituals become a way of linking those who may not have ostensible connections. These poems recall the compositions of the bhakti period when the populist religious movement was a way of mobilizing the people and establishing a sense of unity. Puthuvai does not come across as advocating a Hindu world. Rather, the temple he is familiar with becomes a trope for unity and social integration.

The sense of being human has a great deal to do with accommodating the transcendental. The personal and the public, the private and the social are now able to merge through a consciousness that includes the quotidian and the sacred. Temple rituals and the splendour of deities do not necessarily testify to the richness of a culture. In the failings, opportunism, and the lack of sincerity among devotees, there is something endearing and unfailingly human. As in the medieval bhakti period, for Puthuvai, the temple provides a strategy for confronting the human. The temple acts as a foil to human claims of piety, but the language of Puthuvai's poetry affirms the richness of a culture, even in its failures.

In some ways, the orality of poetry is most easily discernible in Puthuvai's recent work. Sivathamby, in his preface to the recent collection, recalls a moment when he personally witnessed the kind of popular appeal caused by his poetry.[13] And while there is a distinction between such poems and ones that are meant to be read, even in the latter the rhythms are clearly oral in that they draw on folk rhythms. It is almost as if the oral dimension becomes far more noticeable at a time of social and political upheaval. Puthuvai relies heavily on tone and rhythm, with the consequence that language acquires a certain kind of freedom. Simile rather than metaphor is his forte, and often the poems carry themselves forward by the sheer energy of the language. A rich tradition of alliterative verse now re-enters contemporary Tamil poetry through his writings, affirming the significance of the autochthonous at a time of crisis.

A substantial portion of Puthuvai's poems is driven by a desire to extol the militant movement, though admittedly sometimes his ideological stance becomes a noticeable impediment. His best known songs are driven by a rhetoric that is deeply emotional in its appeal. Unlike the poetry of Cheran or Jayapalan, his characteristic mode does not accommodate paradox and ambivalence. The rhythm, the music, and a strong sense of the visual carry forward the momentum of the poems. If this collection does not include such poems it is not because he is not entitled to his beliefs but because they do not go beyond chronicling particular moments or events. It is true that he focuses on the personal in order to access the public, and there is always a sense of immediacy to his tendentious poetry, but in the final analysis such poems are end-stopped.

At their best, however, the political poems are enmeshed in the social and cultural in ways that are clearly revelatory. They do not preach or proclaim. Instead, the world of everyday life gets transformed into something completely different in the most understated way. The diction is simple and the voice not intrusive. The reader sees the familiar world anew and there is no meaning outside the structure of the poem itself. The texture itself is reminiscent of the work of Mahakavi, with the difference that the pathos, agony, and sacrifice of political struggle come across as a revelation. We realize that if Puthuvai gets his inspiration by aligning himself to a political movement, he finds his true voice by looking at what it means to be human in a world torn apart.

Jayapalan began writing at probably the same time that Puthuvai did, although his first collection appeared in 1986. He published another three collections before his collected works, comprising a large number of poems, was published in 2002. His recent collection brings together some of his earliest poems, written in the 60s, and it gives the reader a strong sense of the trajectory of Jayapalan's poetry. Unlike Puthuvai, who was a cultural ambassador of sorts for the LTTE, and Cheran, who is a sociologist and an academic, Jayapalan has remained, for the most part, a poet and nothing else. Surprisingly, very few critical appraisals of his work are available, and even the special issue of the journal *Mallikai* (December 2003) featuring his picture on the cover has only a three-page write-up about him. That brief essay praises him for what he is now best known: his uncompromising stance about the injustice done to the Muslims when they were evicted from the North by the LTTE. His political stance has won him both friends and enemies, but his strength lies not in his political views so much as his remarkable capacity for shaping the conventional lyric into a very contemporary poetic form.

Even his prose is unfailingly lyrical. For instance, here is how he describes the small island of Neduntheevu—off the northern coast of Sri Lanka—where he grew up: "Beautiful beaches, the sight of horses trotting across grassy plains, lands surrounded by stone hedges where the labor of people has created fertile gardens, the sight of beautiful women in the evening, walking in rows, carrying pots to fetch water, villagers versed in a number of crafts—this was my lovely island (*Suriyanodu Pesuthal*, 9)." The images smack of stereotype, but they are consistently redeemed by the language. He adds: "This is where an angel, walking across the dusty streets to collect water, walked across my heart and my poetry, placing the imprint of first love." Language is truth in his poetry. Conventional images are an intrusive presence, and they sometimes have the effect of diminishing the immediacy of his poetry, but in the larger scheme of things, it is a princely failing. He needs the lyrical; in his finest poems, the lyrical impulse transforms the experience in memorable ways.

In retrospect, he could not have sustained the lyricism of his early poetry without the intervention of a turbulent political climate. Jayapalan's activism of the 70s and his sympathies with the oppressed led to a number of poems that are interesting but fail to connect the poetic with the social in any meaningful way. The referent in his early poetry often reflects the artifice of convention rather than a lived reality. To say this is not to discount the sheer power of his poetic language. His imaginative strength and his lyricism have always been evident. Had the political events of Sri Lanka not intervened, he would still have been a major poet, but the poetry would have lacked the sense of a distinctly personal voice. The events of 1983, and the entire experience of exile, brought to Jayapalan's poetry a very different sensibility. The change is most evident in the songs he has written for children. More significantly, it is the rhythms of ordinary speech, the language of everyday dialogue, images that are quotidian, that now get juxtaposed with a language that is poetic in its repetition, its alliteration, and its formal balance. The casualness with which he combines images that are reminiscent of classical Tamil poetry with contemporary tropes contributes to that sense of artlessness and extreme artifice in his work.

Memory is quite central to Jayapalan's poetry. Landscapes, people, and events are often remembered and transformed. Nostalgia and exoticism are constant dangers to poets who suffer displacement. Jayapalan's journey to Norway was a difficult one, via different cities in a number of countries. Each land heightens the sense of dislocation. Whether he speaks of Coimbatore or Oslo, the dominant note is one of regret and longing. In such instances it is the presence of the mundane, the rhythms of ordinary speech that preserve the deep conviction of the poem. Lines such as

> Those from afar,
> now enjoy all;
> those from here,
> now own grief.
> (*Suryanodu Pesuthal*, 42)

are a testimony to the manner in which a poetic idiom suddenly encapsulates the oral to produce a rich texture.

There are at least four distinct phases in Jayapalan's poetry, although such divisions need to keep in mind both continuities and departures. His first phase is that of a nature poet in which the backdrop of an idyllic nature serves to frame human relations in harmony with the rhythms of nature. The second phase begins in the 80s when both the escalation of violence and the increasing tension between the LTTE and the Muslims of the North and East becomes a focal point of his poetry. Deeply sympathetic to the plight of Muslims who were evicted from the North, he writes a number of poems recalling a time of harmony between the two groups.[14] This was also the time he wrote his political and nationalist poems. The third phase begins with his period of exile, first in India and later in Europe. The more recent phase demonstrates a reengagement with "home" but with the changes brought by time and distance.

In fact, even a brief reading of an early poem about the Pali river together with his more recent long poem (which he calls a minor epic) *Ealathu Mannum Engal Muhangallum*, provide a sense of how his poetry has altered over three decades, moving from convention to a distinctly indigenous voice. Naturally the epic poem, stretching to over 3000 lines, affords much greater flexibility. It allows for a narrative involving the poet, a cast of imaginary and "real" characters, and a sequence of events spanning several decades. As the title indicates, it is intended to be the story of our times. The latter is clearly his major work to date, but its significance lies in the ways in which the range of voices—parents, siblings, friends, lovers, oppressors, nature, etc. allow for a language that draws deeply from a number of sources. As with his early poems, it is ultimately nature that defines what it means to belong to a land, and it is nature that becomes a repository of memory. But against this backdrop is a whole saga of human activity, and the diction draws from a range of sources to transform the poem into a contemporary document about love, suffering, and hope. Sometimes the artifice is overt—as when the white horse speaks in English. Sometimes the naturalness masks the artifice, as in dialogue or in folk songs. The transition is reminiscent of the movement of the self-contained lyricism of Sangam literature to the subsequent age of the narrative poem. The analogy is not far-fetched—Jayapalan's engagement with classical poetry is not only evident in his use of tropes, but also in his accounts about his boyhood familiarity with classical poetry. Jayapalan was fortunate in that his parents were lovers of literature. He records with deep gratitude the influence of his parents in shaping his career as a poet.

In his prefatory note to his collected poems, Jayapalan refers to the period 1987-95 as a dark interim. It was certainly not a period of poetic stasis, but it probably was a period of personal uncertainty and conflict. The recent poems may well contain a note of optimism, an assertion of life in ways that may not have been present in his early poetry. But the real shift, ironically, appears to have occurred during this period when his poetic voice changed from a measure of solipsism to one that was more open, more dynamic, and sharply conscious of the need to accommodate the local and everyday into a voice that was both familiar and strange, ordinary and poetic.

Compared to Puthuvai, Jayapalan is much more a poet of personal voice. There is a sense in which he is a flâneur, moving from place to place, speaking to and about his people. There are times when that stance becomes almost a privileged position, as he comments on politics and exile from his own exile in Chennai, Oslo, or Toronto. Very self-consciously, he absorbs many of the foreign landscapes as he looks back on his identity and his home in Sri Lanka. In terms of diction and allusion, then, his recent poems are very different from his early ones. But the continuities are also present.

In one of his self-relexive poems, Jayapalan speaks about his commitment to truth, even if that means taking contradictory positions:

> ask my Sinhalese friends,
> my Muslim brothers and sisters,
> when war descended on me,
> I tried to be human;
> that, then, is my best poem.
> (*Jayapalan Kavithaikal*, 35)

In a general sense, that is true of his poetry. Unlike Puthuvai, who has remained steadfast in his conviction, Jayapalan writes a more open poetry, accommodating different points of view. His strength, however, lies not in his capacity to champion one cause or another but in his extraordinary facility for lyricism and metaphor. Often his metaphors gesture towards an imagined reality. His description of a particular landscape or scene does not always ring true; it is not intended to. What it does, however, is to create a powerful evocation of what has been lost. Even when he speaks of the problems faced by the Muslims in internal exile, it is really the power of metaphor that forces the reader to recognize the trauma of such displacement. Jayapalan's poetry unfailingly invites the reader to enter another world, and it is this world with all its lyricism and metaphor that suddenly forces the reader to acknowledge the flaws and agonies of the real world.

Cheran's intellectual genealogy is a particularly interesting one: he is the son of Mahakavi, arguably one of the foremost poets of the 50s and 60s. Cheran himself acknowledges in an interview the deep impact of his father's poetry, and his own habit of memorizing large chunks of it and reciting them in public places. He also claims that at a certain stage in his career, the influence became less prominent, as his own voice became clear to him.[15] Nonetheless, in any account that relates to Cheran, it is important to reiterate that it was his father who played a major role in steering a tradition of conventional poetry into becoming socially conscious and accommodating the idiom of ordinary speech. Mahakavi's poetry and his plays enabled a distinct break from the tradition of Tamil poetry from Tamil Nadu in that it was neither experimental nor entirely conventional, but was receptive to both in a distinctly Sri Lankan way. It is important to remember that Mahakavi was writing at a time when poetry was still the possession of a small group of writers and critics, and his own accommodation of the local and the folk was shaped within the framework of conventional poetry. Even in a famous poem such as "Therum Thingalum," where the speech rhythms interact most forcefully with poetic diction, the effect of artifice leans towards convention. To say this does not take away from the contribution of Mahakavi: it simply highlights the fact that he belonged to a particular time and a particular place.

Cheran's significance as a poet has been both documented and discussed more fully than perhaps any other Tamil poet from Sri Lanka. He is also perhaps the one best known in India and internationally. Among Sri Lankan scholars, Sivathamby and Sivasegaram have written incisive essays on his poetry, while in Tamil Nadu the major novelists Sundara Ramaswamy and Jeyamohan, among others, have drawn attention to his work. Although he started writing in the mid 70s, he is the product of a time when the political scene was beginning to change rapidly and the cultural forms of representation were becoming a crucial part of the transformation. The transition from one form of writing to another was thus less dramatic in his work than in the writing of Jayapalan and Puthuvai. In addition to being deeply concerned about politics and culture, his poetry was meant for a large readership, without sacrificing a commitment to a noticeable intellectual rigor. To put it differently, the distinctiveness of his poetry lies in his capacity to bring together the traditional and the modern, the lyrical and the intellectual. Even at its most abstract, the poetry retains the tone of oral delivery, while the various tropes insist on a complex train of thought. Cheran's poetry, in addition to being deeply contextual, forces the reader to read carefully and slowly. This could have something to do with his own training in the sciences, or his academic life as a sociologist, but the fact remains that the internal logic of his poems compels the reader to pay close attention to the working of language and metaphor.

Even while making this claim, one needs to be aware that Cheran began writing consistently at a time when students, particularly undergraduates, were deeply preoccupied with the rapid escalation of political conflict. Poetry was seen as an important way of reaching out to the people, and Cheran himself, having grown up with the notion of poetry as performance, was now able to harness this experience and mold it to the new context. His poetry was both recited and performed. And in these instances, passion and lyricism were as important as intellectual rigor. There is a poem in his corpus that is significantly titled, "A Poem That Should Not Have Been Written." It expresses the deep disillusionment of a militant group attacking Sinhalese civilians and the awareness that even the most lofty ideals might mask cruelty. In such poems, the most memorable lines are those that express fierce indignation:

> Beating the drums
> my poetic voice
> proclaimed to all:
> those are unstained hands.
> Now,
> a slap in my face!
> (*Nee Ippozhuthu Irangum Aru*, 118)

If the river is a constant trope in the poetry of Jayapalan, the sea appears time and again in Cheran's poetry. It is not without significance that his very first poem (1975) was titled "Sea." His most recent collection is titled *Meendum Kadalukku* (Back to the Sea), published, coincidentally, soon after the Tsunami hit South Asia. For an island people, it is hardly surprising that the sea is important in both a literal and metaphoric sense. The sea provides freedom and security; it is a protection against outsiders, but it also alienates and makes people insular and vulnerable. The sea takes on a special significance as it embraces various forms of water—rivers, wells, tears, and so forth. His collected poems, published in 2000, has an equally interesting title: *Nee Ippozhuthu Irangum Aru* (The River You Now Step Into), implying the inevitability of change and movement. Writing in the 70s, the sea was benign:

> Evenings caressed by the night,
> the palmyrah leaves then
> lift their heads and sway,
> now the waves rise in
> the caress of the night
> the caress of the night.
> (*Nee Ippozhuthu Irangum Aru*, 24)

In the post-1983 phase, the imagery and the diction change:

> From this shore to the next
> long, heat-carrying tubes
> run across the bottom;

the water torn apart,
icebergs shattered
the path they create
day and night
ships ply the sea.
(*Meendum Kadaluku*, 25)

Between the tragedy of ethnic violence and the sorrow of exile, Cheran finds himself writing a poetry that combines restraint with a deep sense of commitment. In poems such as "Demonic Eyes" the contemporary political scene becomes the occasion for unrestrained satire, looking inward and outward, speaking of the past but foretelling the future. It even invokes the notion of gender without becoming dogmatic in its stance. If Puthuvai turns to the religious, Cheran often alludes to the demonic and the supernatural to find a trope for the excesses that people face all the time. Often the imagery provides a sense of distance, while the rhythms retain that sense of familiarity. As Sivathamby says quite rightly, "Cheran's poetry demonstrates how the new generation recognizes, respond to and understands the experiential changes in society."[16] Negotiating this change is as much about subject matter as it is about style and language. Often the shift in perspective, the movement from one voice to many becomes a strategy for including multiple voices and perspectives.

Cheran's first collection of poems is titled *Irandavathu Soorya Uthayam* (The Second Dawn). Ironically, the second dawn symbolizes the fire that engulfed the Jaffna Public Library when it was burned down in 1981. Since then, with each book, the title has a story to tell. These stories chart the poet's emotional journey through tempestuous times, leading to exile in Canada. The imagination that captures these narratives is often quite startling in its capacity to accommodate the inhuman and the nonhuman. A severed leg or a demonic goddess can become the subject of his poems, but the language remains both grounded and strange at the same time. The reader is often swept along by the rhythm, the repetitions, the refrains, all of which suggest a certain familiarity between the poet and the reader. And yet the structure of the poem is deliberately allusive, moving across time and space, always implying layers of complex meaning. There is an intellectual dimension to his poetry that suggests a genealogy very different from Jayapalan or Puthuvai. In fact, in his critical writing he has advanced the very interesting notion that the social and cultural backdrop of the diaspora needs to be thought of not simply as nostalgia or exile, but as an extension of the tinai concept prevalent in Sangam poetry: in as much as the poetics of the Sangam age was dependent on particular aspects of landscape, so does the poetry of diaspora draw on the specificities of an alien landscape and its social practices. His notion of diaspora as self-sufficient space with its own norms and conventions allows for his poetry to acquire that sense of naturalness while being different. Thus a meeting between the poet and a First Nations Elder is both unusual and predictable. Such poems maintain that balance between the unfamiliar and the familiar that is crucial to his poetry.

Jeyamohan in his essay makes the observation that the poem about the burning of the Jaffna Public Library is among the best that Cheran has written. It is perhaps more true to say that such poems reflect the distinctiveness of Cheran's poetry, what sets it apart from that of many others, including Jayapalan and Puthuvai. His poems draw attention to a political context that is not always overt, but is familiar to those who have some knowledge of the times. Often the references are quite specific to particular moments or events. The poet positions himself as an insider, very much like the informed reader. As the poem progresses, the particular event takes on a symbolic and allegorical dimension. Layers of meaning begin to accumulate, changing the event through an imagination that moves across time and space. The poem itself becomes increasingly allusive until the specific and the general merge, and a particular moment is both fixed in time and timeless in its deeper meanings. As Jeyamohan implies, this is precisely why a poem about a particular time and place transcends its temporal boundaries to become a major work. There is tremendous irony and pathos in calling the burning of a major library a kind of sunrise. But the irony is deliberate. To call it a form of sunset would rob the poem of its urgency, resolve, and optimism.

Cheran's own career during the 80s and 90s often entailed taking oppositional stances. As both a poet and journalist, his views were not always welcome to the state or the various militant groups. His displacement within the country and in Europe was often the result of escaping the wrath of various parties. In such circumstances, the poetry was committed to the particular and the specific. It was hardly possible to be an activist and a poet without invoking the political events of the time. Pathos, outrage, and optimism are all inevitable subjective responses to the constant changes as one scenario gave way to another. Cheran's poems continue to engage us largely because they are shaped by an imagination that goes beyond the immediate. The widespread violence of the '83 pogrom might be the immediate context but the I/eye that perceives the carnage transcends the moment. In the poem "Forgetting" the poet records in minute detail the horror of people being blown apart, but the most tragic moment occurs when a pot of rice is shattered, and a woman's children, hiding in the bushes, are denied their food. Unlike Puthuvai or Jayapalan, understatement is a staple feature of Cheran's poetry. At the most intense moments, the diction gets pared down to essentials. The prose is simple, almost monosyllabic, yet retains its powerful impact.

Both Jeyamohan and Sundara Ramaswamy pay special attention to the presence of love as a dominant motif in Cheran's poetry.[17] A sense of the erotic runs through a number of love poems, which serve to remind us that any serious critical study of Cheran's corpus must recognize that his range is not confined to the political. At the same time it is possible to argue that they often do not resemble conventional love poetry. The exploration of love is framed by a sense of the tragic, suggesting that in a curious way, love and turmoil are two sides of the same coin.

A comprehensive account of the remarkable burgeoning of Sri Lankan Tamil poetry in the last two decades is beyond the scope of this introduction. On the one hand it is strange that poetry should flourish during a time of fragmentation and suffering. On the other, the massive changes that occurred during a short span of time provide the imaginative intensity that poets needed. While it is important to keep in mind the kinds of issues that have given rise to the richly sensitive poetry, it is more important to recognize that the recent flowering of poetry marked a shift from the overtly poetic to the everyday and the quotidian. But this did not entail a drop in aesthetic standards. In fact, the broadening of poetry as a genre to read by all allowed for the recuperation of the oral in a very broad sense. At public meetings, in high school and university settings, in small magazines and newspapers, poetry became a natural presence. A detailed study of the poetry of this period that takes into account the many voices in the different regions and subcultures of Sri Lanka together with the many voices in the diaspora would reveal why the last three decades could well be called the era of Tamil poetry. In no part of the world—and that includes Tamil Nadu—has poetry flourished in the way it has in and among Sri Lankan poets both at home and in the diaspora.

In the poetry of Puthuvai, Jayapalan, and Cheran, this burgeoning of poetry takes three different forms. For Puthuvai, the ordinariness of the sacred becomes an occasion for celebration. The celebration of the everyday is tied in with a commitment to a particular political ideology. The struggle for political autonomy and the celebration of the ordinary complement and complete each other. He has always been a poet with a mission, but his poetry is also about his dedication to his vocation as a poet. Jayapalan and Cheran are equally concerned with the intersection of the personal and the political, but they remain unattached to any particular ideological stance. They share much in common, but as Sivathamby suggests, "unlike Cheran, Jayapalan looks at the 80s while locating himself in the social experience of the early 70s. Cheran, eschewing these experiences, looks at the experience of the new generation from within that framework" (*Tamil*, 98). Jayapalan's political poetry tends to be general in that it hardly ever makes specific reference to groups or movements that are readily identifiable. Political critique in Cheran generally has a specific target, and the educated reader identifies the specific allusions in the poems. Sivasegaram points out in a perceptive review that suffering alone does not ensure good poetry, and that good literature needs to be allusive, not descriptive.[18] But when suffering must be shared with a large reading public, when it must be read in academic settings and in trenches, the form transcends earlier categories and reaches out to accommodate the colloquial, the folk, and the everyday.

The seventy-five poems that have been translated in this collection are, as mentioned earlier, my personal choices. Cheran, Jayapalan, and Puthuvai are, by any standards, major poets, but they are certainly not the only ones. Between a choice of translating a few poems by many poets and translating a substantial body from three poets, the latter seemed to make more sense. Together, they reveal certain trends, certain attitudes to political situations and aesthetic standards. The personal and the public, the sacred and the profane, the political and the aesthetic merge in their writing to force the reader to move beyond narrow affiliations and see the last several decades in all their complexity. In spite of the evocations of turmoil and destruction, there is also a pervasive note of optimism and joy in their poetry. There is a deep conviction that the future will be free of sorrow. Tinged with grief, their poetry and the worlds they create gesture towards a wilting laughter.

CHELVA KANAGANAYAKAM

NOTES

1. The metaphor here is deliberate. In 2009, Penguin India has published an anthology of translations that offers a valuable sampling of Tamil poetry from ancient to modern times. See *The Rapids of a Great River*, ed. Lakshmi Holmstrom, Subashree Krishnaswamy, and K Srilata (New Delhi: Penguin, 2009).
2. See *Kaalam* (December 2008): 24-36.
3. Bharathi (1882-1921) is one of the most influential Indian poets of the 20th century. His powerful poems served as a major incentive for the people of Tamil Nadu to intensify their struggle against British rule.
4. I have used the term Puthuvai to refer to Puthuvai Ratnathurai, since he is best known by that name.
5. Jayapalan and Puthuvai have also lived in the Vanni for a considerable period of time.
6. R Cheran, A Yesurasa, R Pathamanba Iyer, P Nadarasan (eds.). *Maranothul Valvom* (Coimbatore: Vidiyal Pathippagam, 1985).
7. Preface to *Maranaththul*, p. 11. Unless otherwise noted, all the translations of primary and secondary material are mine.
8. A Jesurajah M A Nuhman, ed., *Pathinoru Eazhathu Kavignarkal* (Chennai, India: Cre-A, 1984; 2003).
9. To make this point is not to suggest that one collection is inherently better than the other. In fact, it has been argued that *Maranothul* includes several poems that are tendentious to the point of ignoring aesthetic merit. Nonetheless, the presence of such poems does not invalidate the claim that the collection, taken as a whole, reveals a radical shift in perspective. For an insightful review of the collection, see, S Sivasegaram, *Vimarsanangal* (Madras: South Asian Books, 1995).
10. Jayapalan is the author of five volumes and a complete collection of his poems. The titles are *Suriyanodu Pesuthal* (1987), *Namakkendru Oru Pulveli* (1987), *Ezhathu Manum Engal Mukangazhum* (1987), *Oru Akathiyin Paadal* (1990), *Uyirtheluntha Kavithai* (1998). For his collected works see VIS Jayapalan, *VIS Jayapalan Kavithaikal* (Chennai: Sneha, 2002). Cheran's publications include *Irandavathu Suriya Uthayam* (1983), *Yaman* (1984), *Kaanal Vari* (1989), *Elumbu Koodukalin Urvalam* (1990), and *Erithu Kondirukkum Neram* (1993). For his collected poems, see, R Cheran, *Nee Ippozhuthu Irangum Aaru* (Nagercoil, Tamil Nadu: Kalachuvadu, 2000). His most recent collection is titled *Meendum Kadalukku* (2005). Puthuvai Ratnathurai has published five volumes: *Vanam Sivakkirathu* (1970), *Oru Thozhanin Kathal Kaditham* (1976), *Iratha Pushpangal* (1980), *Ninavazhiya Natkal* (1993), *Viyasanin Ulaikalam* (2003). For his collected poems, see Puthuvai Ratnathurai, *Poovarasam Veliyum Pulunikkunchuhalum* (Jaffna: Nanguram, 2005).
11. Even a sampling of major titles would include, S Sivasegaram, *Poerin*

Muhangal (Colombo: National Association for Art and Literature, 1996), Shanmugam Sivalingam, *Neer Valaiyangal* (Chennai: Tamiliyal, 1988), Solaikkili, *Kalam Kalitha Kanavu* (Adaiyar, Chennai: Ponni, 1991), M Ponnambalam, *Poriyil Akapatta Thesam* (Colombo: n.p., 2002), KP Aravindan, *Kanavin Meethi* (Chennai: Ponni, 1999), Natchaththiran Sevvinthiyan, *Eppothavathu Oru Naal* (Chennai: Thamarai Selvi, 1999), P Ahilan, *Padhungu Kuzhi Natkal* (Erode, Tamil Nadu: Kuruththu, 2000), Sivaramani, *Sivaramani Kavidaigal* (Toronto: Vizhippu, 1994), *Sollatha Sethikal*, (Jaffna, Sri Lanka: Women's Study Circle, 1986), A Mangai, ed. *Peyal Manakkum Pozhuthu* (Chennai: New Book Lands, 2008), R Murugaiyan, *Naangal Manithar* (Chennai: National Art and Literary Association, 1992).

12. This interview has not been published.

13. Says Sivathamby: "In order to recognize the full impact of Puthuvai's poetry, they need to be heard as songs. I have witnessed the most ordinary people listening to his poetry with rapt attention" (21).

14. It must be mentioned that in terms of quality, his broader political poems outnumber those that are directly concerned with the eviction of the Muslims.

15. For the complete interview, see *Kalachchuvadu* (July-Sept. 99): 11-32.

16. See K Sivathamby, *Tamil Elakkiath Thadam* 1980-2000, Colombo: Moonravathu Manithan, 2000: 101

17. For Sundara Ramaswamy's essay, see *Kalachchuvadu*, 32 (Nov-Dec, 2000): 210-14.

18. See *Vimarsanangal*, 33.

R Cheran

MY LAND

A net spread across the shallow waters
the heavy breath of the wind above,
from the middle of the ocean,
fingers pressing down

the unruly hair,
we look up
see the shore,
palmyrah trees, and sporadically,
the tiled roofs.

The waves,
the spray and
the roar of engines
the ninety minutes
how did they end?

Later, an expanse of sand
the rooted
palmyrah trees,
each the height of a man,
on that virgin sand;
the sand itself,
buried mirrors
where the sun settles;
reflections of gold;
beneath that
two thousand years ago
my ancestors walked
this earth;
one footstep
a thousand years;
our roots are deep.

Sleepless, one woman
standing on these shores,
lamenting the stars

falling into the sea;
or another, waiting for
the horizon to split apart,
bring her boat home;
on their bare breasts
trinkets in which, or
in the footprints
now covered by sand
that late evening, with
coconut trees swaying in the wind,
my ancestors
have left a message
for me.

On a hundred thousand shoulders
I stand
this is my land, I shout;
across the seven seas
defying the rising waves
the wind carries
this voice:

My land
My land.

THE PAST

A deserted street,
in the rain,
in the canopy of a tree,
suddenly

to see you
seemed unlikely, but
it did happen.

After so long,

your eyes fluttering,
coloured butterflies
grasping an umbrella,
and a bundle of books.
I see the trembling fingers,
you were stunned.

Face,
you cannot turn away,
rain;
leaving,
not possible,
rain.

Rain, go away;
Sun, come again,
you seem to chant to yourself,

my little girl,

the Sun
of our past
on that day,
disappeared.

TO A SINHALESE GIRL

You have heard
we come from far way,
beyond the horizon
where bullets are sown
in fields
not grain,
where plush houses abound
and terrorists breed;
your surprise
at meeting me

an ordinary man,
will soon fade from you
and your friends.

On the banks of Palaavi
now the colour of muddied sand;
yet another
as the clouds
spread a blanket of shade
on the muddied water;
the canopy of the moon
finely embroidered
to make the water glitter;
seated on the ghat,
I listen
to the melody
of your Sinhala songs
and my heart melts.

Once in the past,
A boy then,
at the Maho station
while waiting with my father
for the train,
walking along the tracks
at midnight
in low tones
a lullaby wafted
across.
The child's sniffles
and the lilting song
that night
pierced my heart;
I was saddened.

A gentle grief
surrounds me
today.

Till end of July
a gusty wind;
in the blowing wind
the ponnochi flowers
shed their petals;
the long-feathered peacock
flustered
as its step falters;
from relishing these sights
with a smile,
do our languages
separate us?

To please you,
I cannot even
pluck a feather from
the peacock for you;
in the early evening
on the grassy plain
under a full moon
in spite of your wish
I couldn't accompany you.

Your eyes will not forget
these mild disappointments;
and I could not forget
your gentle love.
Without strangling nature
we let the flowers bloom
the grass grow,
we left.

You to the south
me going north
in the dawn
when from the mountains
from above the trees
a gentle breeze
descends;

when brushing your teeth
while meandering
in the midst of your work
seeking to reclaim
the city
you will remember
our brief encounter.

Tell your people,
here too
the flowers bloom
the grass grows
and birds fly.

NOT PARALLEL WORLDS

Two girls,
two goats.

They cross
a harvested field,
walk eastward;
more fields in the east,
stretches and stretches of bunds
blue expanding to blue skies.

Yellow flowers in bloom;
from chanal bushes
mynah birds
emerge to gently fly away.

Two girls,
one younger,
the other gently smothered
in youth;
front and rear,
walked two goats.

They pause,
rub their backs in the grass
and continue.

In the horizon, shedding
long parallel lines
a plane arose;
seeing it rise,
the four eyes in the field,
scan the expanse of sky;
in the quiet plains
a gentle shudder.

The plane climbs higher
the parallel lines stretch further;
the evening breeze ruffles their hair
along the bunds they journey on.

Two girls,
two goats.

RITUAL

Later,
they all sat down;

In the centre
of a courtyard house
a long table,
covered with cloth;
the land transferred,
the house given away,
pictures taken,
money counted
heads nodding,
that too photographed;

in large ledgers,
they stoop to sign;
next the exchange of rings.

Then,
all sat down,
on the floor.

Evening isn't it?
A meal of idli,
bawling kids
settling to sleep,

then,
he sat by her side again,
more friendly now;
"He".

SUMMER FIELDS

The long bunds
criss-cross the fields.

The chanal tree spreads
above the bund,
yellow flowers cover the fields;
on the ghats of the temple pond
the sheep graze,
the spreading branches of the tree,
a hammock from a branch.

The cry of a child;

abandoning the planting
she gave her breast to the child;

the betel-filled mouth

glistening red

she returns to the field
again,
the cry of a child.

THE SECOND SUNRISE

On that day,
there was no wind;
no rising tide,
even the waves had died.
Sea.

Walking across,
feet sinking in the sand,
again a sunrise.

This sunrise in the South.

What happened?
My town was burned;
my people became faceless;
in my land, my air,
in everything,
the stamp of outsiders.

Hands clasped behind you,
who do you wait for?
On the clouds
fire
has written its tale;
who waits even now?

From the ashen streets,
arise and march.

TWO MORNINGS AND A LATE NIGHT

Today, this is how
it dawns:
the night still lingers,
the light's expanse muted,
at this time;
to wake and step out
when the koel sings
from the branch of a well-side tree;
below the earth,
deep and broad,
the well
sleeps peacefully,
like my heart.

Today, this is how
it dawns.

Do not think
it will be such dawn again
tomorrow;
halfway through the night,
at the gate,
the deep growl of the jeep,
the clatter of boots;
with a shudder
the doors of our house
spread open;
then
eyes half-closed and tired
having studied
for the exam next day,
in that night

we hear "their" call;
the howling wind
in our ears.
"Where he is?" they ask

their broken Tamil
pierces the heart.

Speechless
stunned,
as we shake our heads
flung into the jeep
the running engine
still growling.

What then?
It is life
as usual.

The morning sun
on bare earth
above me
grass.

Sometimes coming home
wanting to announce
before opening the door,
turning aside
to hawk and spit,
from inside
the sound of amma's cough.

I waited
to open the door.
the world outside
as before
lay calm.

YAMAN

The wind falters
as fear
fills the night;
I gasp
at the stillness
between the stars.

Whose shadow lurks by the door?

I wouldn't know,
nor would they;
it happened
swiftly.

Death.

No reason
no justice
values and virtues
freeze where they stand
in the oppressive silence.

In the dark
lost in flight
pigeons
pound and pound again
against the door;
my resolve to endure
slips.

Do the butterflies
disdaining life
shed their colours
in the prime of youth?

As sunflowers
their golden petals

untouched by dust,
lotus flowers
that bloom at the
touch of water;
as stars,
they will be
born again;
until then
at the edge of the lake,
stare at the waves.

DEMONIC EYES

She wakes
from a dreamless slumber;
three pm.

Half the world she sees.

A goblet that fell
as she kicked
the defiant lover
lies upturned on the floor.

Sardonic, she smiles
observing
the sprouting grey hair
that refuses to be dyed.

As she yawns
the clothes slip
for just a moment
a sliver of light enters.

Darkness again,
her demonic lids droop
her legs falter

her fingers shake.
The cell phones
of ministers waiting from dawn
now silent,
emptiness looms in
the advisory hall.

They can neither wait
nor, tired of waiting,
leave, a dilemma
that is the sycophant's reward.
She comes;
drunk no more,
but the eyes remain clouded;
those who sang
"Even the flowers swooned
at the rustle of her dress"
now discreetly move away.

The words
that described her as goddess
now fill those sewage pits;
the arrogance fed
by her father and mother,
by the grandparents,
echoing in the harsh
steps of her feet;
followed by her captain
who has no legs himself.

"Can you match
the scale of my destruction?"
Unable to oppose
her words,
the former leaders
now hide their faces.

Home, land, and country
a massive mirror reflecting

none but her beauty—
a madness
hers.

A breast wrenched and flung
can burn a city;
fearing the worst,
breasts of women, in the North and East
she explodes
and destroys.

The demon goddess
of a history that repeats
not laughter but blood itself;
she laughs, scattering pain
she glares, causing grief
she walks, creating hell!

FORGETTING

We can forget all;
spurning the loss
of this miserable life,
with the confidence
sparked in a moment;
along Galle road,
we race
with pounding hearts;

jutting from the burning car,
a thigh bone;
fixed on a spot
between the earth and sky
a staring eye;
no eye, but the socket
filled with blood,
on Dickman's road;

instead of black heads
bloodied remants
of six men;
a piece of cloth
escaping the fire,
severed,
without a watch
a lonely left arm;
from the burning house
carrying the weight
of a cradle
a pregnant Sinhalese woman,

all these,
all these can be forgotten.
But,
that late evening
when the clouds
descended to conceal
the tea bushes
where you hid your children,
when, after so long
with the little rice
in the pot
you waited, hiding
for the rice to cook
you were shattered.
How can I forget,
the broken pot,
the scattered rice?

DEATH OF A DAY

Every day
in the night
when all sleep
and dogs cease to bark,

only the stars now alone
with the sky,
I go to sleep.

In a crowded street,
unable to run,
not knowing how to sit,
breathless and faltering;
such a dream
halfway through the night,
I wake up.

Sometimes
the sea and river turn yellow
and November flowers
unfold;
I dream of walking.

I wake in the morning
my hands in one place
legs in another,
even my face
scattered elsewhere.

I gather and connect them,
stand upright
and my day
I sell to you.

THE STORY OF A SEVERED LEG

I am writing the story of a severed leg.

A road that begins in the mountains
runs through this barren land
to the city,
now lies distraught.

The story of war mixed with blood
in scattered fragments
like restless ghosts,
follow the road in grief.

The tears of wounded trees,
settle on the marks
left by vehicles
of well-meaning NGOs.

The dust covers the tears,

indifferent, like an undertaker
covering the body
of an unclaimed corpse.

Dismembered by war,
the road survives;
I saw;
where the road forks,
a half-broken milestone;

on it sat
a skull.

On this barren road
consumed with thirst
turning towards the forest,
I saw,
beneath the Palai tree
a severed leg.

A thousand stories
rose to fill the forest
from that leg
lying without protest.

Those stories displaced

the wondrous tales and visions
the forest acquired at birth,
long before memory's time.

The displaced stories and beliefs
in diasporic lands
in the temples of Tamils,
in their myriad lives,
now hang,
embodiments of sin.

Beneath those,
compassion in darkened rooms,
the irresponsibility of distance,
I see
in these walking corpses.

I saw
in the forest engulfing
pain, courage, sorrow, oppression,
despair—the severed leg.

I saw,
on the tomb of my dreams,
scattering its stories
in silence,
the severed leg.

VIMALATHASAN, MY BROTHER

This letter
will not reach you
I harbor no such illusions.
But
I cannot help but write;
My heart
beats,

a butterfly's wings.

Do you remember
when I last
met you?
On that day,
you without
your shoulder bag;
lots to talk,
nothing was possible
in all that haste.
I have lost weight
you told me,
(everyone says that).

But,
look who is talking?

Here,
the situation is bad.

For us to live
the essentials
have dwindled
perilously.

In the nights
almost everyone
sees horrible dreams.
In those,
flying upside down
helicopters,
armored vehicles
driving over
children.

Our children
make paper guns
and play.

At times,
when all shops
close
in the city,
the coffin maker
alone
with confidence
displays his wares.

Do you know
I wonder,
we lost
many dear friends
how would I describe
how that happened?

Yet,
"nature abhors a vacuum"
this you know,

until the end
we will
stay our course.

LETTERS FROM AN ARMY CAMP

Dear Nanda:

arrived this morning,
no problems;
I could hardly sleep,
while gripping the rifle
on my lap;
horrible dreams,
I kept waking
with a shudder.

You and your mother
wept bitterly
at the station;
I too was scared,
but
what I was told
about the North
was not true;
As in every place,
shops, streets
throng of vehicles,
but people avert their eyes,
if they happen to look
I see in their eyes
something,

a flicker,
its meaning
I don't understand.

You know
we cannot
travel by ourselves;
two armoured vehicles
two jeeps or
three;
a truck
fifty of us at least
travel together
that is really a parade;
you would have seen
on independence day
just like that;
one difference,
in that parade
we were free
our guns empty,
now,
we have bullets
are no longer free.

2.
Today was exhausting,
on the winding road
(they are terrible)
between the palmyrah trees
the armored vehicles jolting
the bones in my back
hurt so much.

Midday,
in a village
among the fields
we shot
three fat goats;
no young men around,
the women ran and hid;
halfway on our return,
someone remembered
we hadn't bought
cigarettes
for the Major.
What then,
the entire convoy
now wound its way
back to the city.

3.
Today
Edirweera and Chandrasiri
shot and killed three Tamils.
"in a crowded street
suddenly they ran,
confused, I shot them"
explained Chandra.
Later,
no inquiry
both sent to Colombo
transferred
(lucky ones).

Shoot someone
attack the public
set fire to homes
an immediate transfer.

Yesterday,
five were transferred,
since I arrived
fifty at least
have returned;
when would I be
transferred,
I don't know.

4.
Today one hundred
soldiers
joined our camp.
Youngsters,
hardly a moustache,
not even trained
to handle machine guns.

Now
even after roaming
during the day,
the night brings
no sleep.
So long
since I saw you,
but asking for leave
unthinkable.

5.
Last night
"they" killed
thirteen of us;
with deadly accuracy,

a bomb exploded
followed by machine guns
that surrounded us;
no one expected this;
In spite of constant
radio contact
with the main camp
no escape
As Yaman descended
in the night.

The next morning
no one on the streets
no shops;
a strange silence,
what is this land?

Now
the nights are cruel,
as moonlight spreads
shadows move
suddenly,
strange birds screech,
hell until dawn.

Later
having asked for
immediate transfer,
our division
took to the streets;
how many were killed
we are not sure
fifty or sixty
Major says.

6.
Dear Nanda
finally it ended;
tomorrow my transfer,

thank God.
Today I went
for the last time
to the city;
Nothing terrible,
as before, shops and streets
the people
as before,
avert their eyes.

THE GHOST`S SONG

Guns on both sides
me in the middle
an innocent commoner
that is my name.

I have no city
I did;
now it is gone
(thanks to holy India!)

Guns on both sides
me in the middle;
a burning fire
me in the middle.

He says "sit"
the other says "stand";
he says "go"
the other says "come".

He said "die"
another said "live";
he slew the body
another killed the soul.

And I became
a ghost.

ROAMING

We sit across from each other.
the windows become wings,
as the train races;
disturbed,
the butterflies flutter;
fields pass by,
reappear.

Still,
the sea is lovely, the mountains are lovely;
the river too is lovely.
All,
in our posture,
gather meaning.

A PROCESSION OF SKELETONS

His dreams
are ordinary;
the palmyrah dreams
of the Jaffna middle-class.

The palmyrah seed grows;
becomes a fence,
then grows further,
a tree and a larger fence;
it survives patiently;
twenty years
it grows firmly
unchanging.

Until then, waiting
a patient sacrifice.

He studies

late into the night,
until he sleeps
his mother is awake,
to nudge, to offer tea
to unclasp the hold of night.

If mother cannot,
then the sister
older or younger.

The years accumulate.

Medicine, engineering, commerce
the triumvirate;
now add computers,
an additional deity
to the three gods.

In some ways
the palmyrahs and the studies
are sturdy.
the survival of the fittest
the death of the weakest,
thanks to Darwin;
let this bolster
science,
not society.

But
the palymyrah does not
know to thrive;
to give it nourishment,
the air, the night, the moon
sometimes even
gentle music
are needed.

If not for these
would life not waste away?

His dreams are ordinary;
to flourish,
they do not know.

One day
his dreams were transformed.

In those,
a procession of
skeletons
male skeletons
female skeletons
skeletons of kids
skeletons carrying babies
young skeletons,
old skeletons
even without arms;
eyes fixed,
in the same direction
from frozen sockets
streams of blood and tears.

Thousands of them
skeletons in line;
on them
eyes filled with hate
the soldiers
used their guns.

On one side
turbaned soldiers,
the stench of Nijam arecanut
peanut oil
ghee
a half-smoked beedi,
surrounding them;
also,
those with black scarves
around their heads.

On the other
washed clothes and looking trim
in shining Japanese vehicles
soldiers.

Yet another side,
the local army
their guns
now turned elsewhere.

Bullets
pierced the skeletons
and went afar.
Despite the distance to travel,
the skeletons
began to emerge;
defying the bullets
trampling the tanks
stepping on
the scattering soldiers,
they walked,
their procession unending,
fearsome.

Having woken from the dream,
he realized that the scattered pieces
lay on the banks of the Seine,
under the sky track of Wuppertal,
in the snowy terrain
of Toronto.

Now awake,
he still hears
the sound of marching
skeletons.

GRAVE SONG

He by himself,
three of them,
impenetrable darkness,
like their hearts.

The torment
of digging
his own grave;
he then understood
a violence
beyond words.

On that grave
in the air,
frozen
his final words.

The wind will not
scatter it,
the rain and sun,
will not dare approach it.

His unsaid words
entered the earth
passed from earth to tree,
then to branches,
finally to leaves,
and now in the wind
they rise in waves
unceasingly.

On that grave
there is no ghost,
no god either,
this is no memorial stone.

Like a solitary lamp

in an empty street,
one stray flower;
on that
time has left
its cruel fingers.

In his final words
lay
the life of our land.

CLOSURE

That night,
a deep blanket of darkness,
shrouded the land;
also,
without the memory of light,
the palms swayed,
a child cried,
the wail of a distant train,
nothing, an unwritten grief.

Listen,
before the people,
told me this
just another story,
that night I felt this grief;
surprising, isn't it?

For people without faces or eyes
his death
was just another occurrence,
something to talk about
until they fall asleep.

Tonight is unlike then,
the moon-splattered leaves

float on the walls,
no flying insects
in the lamp-less streets;
when I began to write,
the faceless ones had
gone to sleep.

That night,
when I went,
to the hospital
outside the gate, a few stood
their heads bowed.

I walked gingerly inside
across the hospital,
tiptoed up the stairs,

ward number 18;
a few beds even on the verandah
lamp light, white uniforms,
you were laid out.

A white cloud from top
to the edge of the bed,
she lifted the sheet
showed me your body,
another tilted your face
with the edge of her palm;
in that one instant,
my heart froze;
beneath my feet,
the world split and sank.

How did this occur?

Your upright walk, twirled
moustache, wavy locks,
I remember;
where the fences lead,

towards the cemetery,
in the east among palmyrah trees,
your goats stray,
and you follow, whistling,
I remember.

Trees
splitting asunder
the chest of the red earth
grow their roots;
the tip of the spike
that uproots them,
how did it enter
your chest?

Those early days
were still in my heart.

Scouring Ilanthai trees,
convinced that golden beetles
would glitter;
the traps for pigeons,
snare the neighbor's fowls,
all these you knew;
seated on the ghats
of the Pillayar temple
time and again,
munching nuts,

lying on grass,
a carpet rolled out for you,
suspecting next-door Chandran
to be a eunuch
dragging him to the bushes,
pulling off his cloth
rushing back
amazed,
how could I forget these?
You went west,

I traveled east,
my friend, today,
I have to see you like this,
blood, flesh,
guts and bones.

That day,
stretching its bones to the sky
a dead giant tree,
your house stood gutted;

your house they burned in the night.

The sun split
into streams of blood;
the flames shooting between
the roof;
we watched from the roof.

They took your land,
today,
you were killed;
they killed you.

Today,
I relive that tale,
the sun alone
no people on these plains,
the lapwing's cry of death,
they returned
after burning you,
later we too
came back.

In this land,
where Nerunji blooms yellow
you don't own
a handful of earth;
your father,

from the Palmyrah
slipped and fell,
in a moment,
he lost his voice and froze;
his father
when he died, was
buried deep
so fruits could thrive;
today, there is nothing,
they cut you up;
when a thousand fingers
tips of rifles
stretched towards you
in the barren Jaffna land
you walked upright.

You were killed;
they killed you.

An unwritten tale;
on this land,
struck by grief,
streaming blood,
paddy grows; chanal flowers bloom,
rain pours.

Sleep well,
outsiders have arrived;
of that,
I must remind them.

ENDING PATHWAYS

In that wide expanse,
two palmyrah trees
hold up the sun;
fallen between them

a narrow pathway
now sundered.

From here,
not even traces remain.

In the hot wind
always blowing towards
the destroyed house,
the wail of a dead sea.

The desolate days will end,
the waste land will thrive,
we hope,
floating on fire, then
walking back home;

landmines everywhere,
no place to step,

was it here,
or there,
that margosa tree?

A shelter,
by its side,
a water trough,
a little further
a rubbing stone
for cattle;

who will speak for these?

to shout aloud,

even the earth disdains,

say some in derision,
I hear their voice.

THE ELDER

I stand alone
in a desolate expanse of snow.

My soles sore and bleeding,
wearing thick shoes
the city in its huge factories
makes and churns out.

Knowing how unsettling
the sight of blood can be,
fearfully,
reluctantly,
I inspect my soles.

They reveal nothing,
flinging back
unanswerable questions.

Ahead
mountains of snow,
hanging streamers of glass
speak to me:
"Pierce me
and pass through
hidden truths will emerge."

I stand alone
in a desolate expanse of snow.
No one to hear
the cry of desolation;

no words to offer
comfort on a solitary path.

Suddenly he appears,
across my path;
gray long hair

studded with snow
eagle feathers around his neck.

Colours drawn across
his face and chest,
a bowl of fire in his hands,
he comes: the Elder.

He makes a small fire;
with feathers
warmed by the flames,
he strokes my soles;
the pain, the blood and the numbness
disappear.

I fling my shoes away.

"Scatter your angry songs,
they will ignite;
walk on the fire
and cross this plain."

He walks away.

His hair waves
in the cold air;
smiling,
I look at my soles.

LOVE SONG

Leaves fall and fall
as winter's slumber approaches;
on cold-smitten trees
breathes
the nascent moon.

In the Hague
along this Parallel Weg
house number 273
the front room;
somewhat newer
Van Gogh's Flowers
on the wall.

The night lamp's gentle light
seeps and falls
on the brassiere
draped
on the back of the chair.

Lips touch
behind ears,
the heart melts
the body unwraps
sparks ignite
a fire.
We exploded into a forest fire;
the snow outside
melts in the
heat of our passion.

Language
consumed by eyes and body;
later
words froze
then
melted and whimpered;
the silence in between
expands
forever.

A rising flood
a moving river
expands into a sea.

A broken, lifeless
alarm
its minute parts,
little twigs scattered
in the fall,
with these lie amok
the senses.

Cupid's mines
exploding life,
love
begins again.

One moment of dissolution
I became a woman.
As you entered me
my senses swooned,
defying gravity;
an endless waterfall
I recognize myself,
become a man.
the night's music,
two lives
in a dance
outside;
a bright moon
twigs still fall.

A bamboo forest
caught in a gale,
the hair asunder
lust burning night.

As it dawns
the fire subsides,
the body hot
Drowsy and restless
yet,
sleep not today
but tomorrow.

Until then
the turning globe on its axis
continue to turn;
the brightening eyes and body
continue to flower.

THE GIANT TREE IN THE RAIN FOREST

A wondrous landscape
where mountain, rain forest and ocean
merge,
the weather mild,
I stand, on
the moist earth.

The imprints of
a swelling ocean draw
patterns on the sand;
even now

a heavy fog
smothers the ocean, slowly;
where the sea ends and land begins
blurred in this magical moment;
the lighthouse siren blares
intermittently,
to guide the confused canoes.
The fog now swallows
the mountains and the forests.

Towering four hundred feet,
having survived the axe of Columbus
having lived a thousand years,
the cedar, now threatened by a fog;
does this presage a battle?

Marked by the wisdom of time

the giant tree smiles,
embraces the fog.
I stand below.

The life of the forest in its roots
the soul of the air in its crown,
the tree,

no tongue to speak,
but in its breath
the tale of history.

Its patience
having vanquished the earth
having spurned the hills,
the giant tree
now flings a branch
to appease the enraged wind.

And below
with chain saws
petty humans stand.

NINE DAYS

I flew
to a new land with a foreign tongue;
a blue wind swept across;
relishing that language
I scattered ten songs.

unblinking eyes,
feet that do not touch the ground,
I walked and flew.

The people of this land,
failed to see my face;

the wind was bemused
by my song;
yet,
angry and gentle,
in the grip
of a swirling passion
it embraced me.

The first three days in the light
the next three days in the dark,
the last three days in tears,
destiny shaped my love.

Forever moist,
no ebb in my kisses,
without feet,
I am in constant flight.

She,
in the city's constant jolts,
in the thorns of time,
the tresses
of an entangled wind.

VIS Jayapalan

GENTLY FLOWS THE RIVER

Scattered among the plains
here and there
fields are ploughed.
The din of machines
hardly dispels
the silence.

With hardly a ripple
the Pali river
flows gently;
the tall weeds
whisper to the winds,
talk incessantly;
the birds
with their music
and the fish
splash as they play.

Still something sustains
the silence;
beyond the bend,
hidden by a rock
amidst the weeds
in the sand
where the Marutha tree
shapes a fence,
filtering the light,
the winsome girls
from our village
gossip with relish
the village news;
they laugh and giggle
tease and scold
wash and bathe.

Yet, silently,
the river moves;

the footprints of
Pandara Vanniyan
are still visible;
here he rested
conferred with his troops
planned his attack,
then washed his dusty feet
drank from the river,
content in the thought
of the retreating British;
he rested awhile
shaded by the same
tree.

Beyond the bend,
in the same enclave,
the women
still bathe,
with hardly a ripple
the river moves on.

SPEAKING TO THE SUN

Eyes open,
the day begins.

Outside the moving bus
our world, forever young;
yellow face glowing,
a Chinese goddess,
from the heavens,
the Sun now arrives.

In our village streets,
skirting sugar cane fields,
in the refuse of
iron factories,

the people raise their heads;
in their path
you dispel the dark
give them hope.

Yesterday at dawn,
in the forests of my land,
with my friends,
I encountered you.
In the early evening
yesterday,
in the darkening sea
on a struggling boat,
I rejoiced seeing
your departing face.

This morning
in Tamil Nadu,
you kissed me
through the window
of a moving bus;
I opened my eyes and
in my hands
a new day
your gift.

A flower in the midst of
fire, we survive in war,
to our lives
I dedicate this day.

To recover that time,
once more,
to stand on our feet
in our shores
and see you,
I dedicate this day.

DAWN

A map spread out
for soldiers to read;
in front of me, a valley;
lakes, streets,
dense homes,
Kandy stretched out,
glitters gently.
Still dark,
the distant mountain tips;
in the tea bushes,
like moving land mines,
carrying baskets,
young girls pick buds;
with leaves and grass,
with flowers, a tapestry
woven by the rains,
now absent,
but even in this spring
like the girls plucking leaves,
the mountains wear a green rag;
a smothering fog,
like scholars pleased
to have swallowed whole
budding young minds;
a smothering fog.
Now the mountain top
lifts its head
scattering the fog;
the koel sings its praise.

THE FENCES IN OUR VILLAGE

On summer days,
all sides of the swept yard,
new colours, new sounds.

Below the heavens,
from sky to earth,
birds rehearse their songs;
flowers let drop
their fragrant slips and
smile;
be it the sky or land,
be it the sea,
April days,
the soul takes flight.

To escape the heat
in our village,
the old ones,
their faces covered with the dust
of old account books,
meet under the Bo-tree.

About the height of their fences,
about the chasteness
of their women,
now turning grey
behind the fences,
about their seeking
gold flowers atop mountains,
how much they brag!

Tear down the kitchen fence
in the plains
the flowers are in bloom.

FOREST AND CITY

In a land
a forest,
in the city a king
his people and his troops;
in the forest,
a man with a moustache.

Forever scared,
hiding behind trees,
no hat to wear
no tomorrow,
he has not heard
the nightingale sing
the monkeys dance.

He
stole a sandalwood tree;
the troops attacked
the people of
Sandalwood city;
then he smuggled ivory,
the troops
attacked the people;
he crossed the boundary
the alien troops
now attacked the
moustache-man's people;
then he walked
along a mountain path
the troops now ripped
the clothes off
mountain women.

The king's troops
at gun point
now chased the people;
the people need a king;

if there is no king,
they need one better,
a warrior.

The people of Sandalwood city,
the people of Elephant city
the moustache-man's people,
the hill country people
all their unending tears,
the troops do not see,
the king
who sent the troops
does not see.

The anger of the people,
a treasure
for the moustache man;
the hate of the people,
becomes a scepter
for the moustache man;
in the emerald forest,
flourishing on tears
rises a palace;
the newly crowned
moustache man
now loves the songs of birds,
dances with the peacocks,
sleeps without fear,
smiles in his dreams.

As the people
shed tears,
the emerald forest grows,

as the emerald forest grows,
the palace gathers strength.

DUALITY

When I was small,
the world was flat.
A giant known to my grandmother
rolled up the world like a mat
and hid it, apparently.
Then,
during the days,
my grandmother waited
looked for the sun
in his seven-colour horse chariot
she prayed, I did too.

One day in class
my lovely teacher
drew a round globe
set it free in the universe;
the sun she took down from the chariot,
placed it firmly in the universe.
Later in school
the teachers placed
so many suns in the universe.

Thus in my
grandmother's world
life was imagined;
in the learned world
my thoughts armed themselves;
these two worlds
in the river of my life
remain opposing shores.

At one end,
long, long ago
for speaking the truth,
a poor woodcutter
received an axe of gold,
a gift from a goddess;

at the other
man is cloned
by scientists.

Rudderless now,
hands sheltering a flame,
in my wanderings
beliefs and science.

PRAYER

I am an ant
with a song;
on the branches
in the honey-dripping
sandalwood forest,
an ant with a song
of faith.

Sharing flowers and wine
in the Spring,
joyfully walking on the streets,
harvesting the god's land
in summer time,
filling our barns
mating in our fragrant homes,
during the rains,
hugging and kissing our fruits
to clothe our nights,
laughing with the young
in the cold,
waiting for sweet-smelling
wind of Spring,
we did nothing else O Allah,
we did nothing else O Jesus,
we did nothing else O Siva,
we did nothing else O Buddha.

O god,
why did you pluck our poems,
fill us with dirges?
If there is rain,
we can hide our eggs
in high land and wait;
why did you send a rain of fire,
why did you soak us in blood?
In our burning streets,
like cats with their young
we wander in
the land, the forest and the sea,
we carry the eggs and flee,
why did you make us fall
at the feet
of tyrants and criminals?
Why did you make us
food for their aluminum
eagles?

Why did you make us scatter,
dust on the world's streets?

To make it worse
we trip among ourselves
we bite and spew each other
why did you clothe our streets
in darkness?

O God,
if you desire, take us,
save our eggs,
let them live.
"we will die
to dispel the darkness,'
say our young
as they perish,
and we watch;

have we lived
to witness this?

"Dharma will triumph"
you proclaim,
taking our lives;
how much longer this torment,
how much longer this oppression,
how long this darkness
how far away
our promised land?

A POEM IN BLOOD

Fifteenth of May
in the India ocean,
screams shatter the sky;
no, not the black sea
stirred by the storm;
you know what I mean,
my dear island people!
That day the glittering red
on my shores,
neither flags nor streamers,
the blood from our
severed heads.

Eyes wide and faces pinched,
in the bitten tongues,
the songs written in blood
let me sing them;
these I have heard
in the village songs
my ancestors,
who fought the Portuguese
and lost, sang.

Like our defiant youth,
among the sand covered stones,
the black palymyrahs
shook their heads and danced;
in the salt heaps,
the migratory birds
screeched.

Terrifying the Dutch
who scorched the cotton fields
for plains for their horses,
my ancestors sang these songs,
I hear them now.

Why does the world remain silent?

You lost face,
my dear people;
recover the face of
my ancestors;
The Pandavas fight
among themselves,
the people of Kurushetra
rise.

(On May 15, 1985, in Nedunteevu, the Navy attacked a boat carrying passengers, and killed more than forty people. This poem is a tearful response to the incident.)

OUR LAND AND A LOVELY SPRING

Chennai's outskirts,
an expanse
of structures,
concrete hives.

In single file

a multitude of people,
wandering file folders
during the day;
in the evening
within those files
numbers and tasks
the working life of a
great city.

For me a solitary Lankan
a late dew in the evening,
I look out the window,
watch a few trees,
listen to a few birds;
like these birds,
I too lived in my land;
after the rains,
in full bloom
my forests;
in Spring my rivers,
rubbing against the grass;
my seas washing the edge
of their garments
on the pebbles of the shores;
giving me the grains,
the fields become grass
for grazing;
a breeze to soothe
our sorrows;
my boys and girls
unfazed by toil and work
embracing life
in the shadow of trees,
singing their songs;
would I live an exile
having lost all these?
My land where
the fallen enemies
decay and rot,

the fallen friends,
heroes to be hailed
rise in their tombs,
how much longer
the infamy and shame?
How much longer
the oppression and death?
Again
in my land
I need my Spring.
In the shadow of
flowering trees, or
in the soil under the grass
rifle clad
I must have my Spring.

MARINA`S GRIEF

The fisherman's blood
crying for justice
now kissed by the wind
from the Bengal sea;
the son of the soil
always cursed
with blood and death;
why this grief
wherever I go?
Why am I beset
with despair?
Moving beyond burnt buses
beyond a moving khaki fence
this expanse of the universe
on Marina's sand I plant my feet.

Today the cars do not roar;
no sign of philistine obesity;
a beautiful Marina

now grief-stricken,
blood-stained grief;
Is this the fate of man?
I ask with abject tears.

"Don't go there," a moving
fence commanded;
"fishermen are dangerous"
it warned, its
breath smelling of blood.

A tone I once had heard;
for Lankans a familiar voice;
the same voice of white wolves
the children of the States
who slaughtered Indians.
The voice of those
white hunters who killed
the aborigines of Tasmania;
here the skin was brown;
I walked back in despair.

What does it mean,
beautifying the beach?
Home, water and school
for the fisher folk?
Or kill and bury them?
I walked back in despair.

When the fishermen's blood
mixed with the dust
maybe the bells were silent!
where flags and cries and hands
rented the sky,
maybe the white doves flew!

LAND OF THE SINGING FISH

For the sea of Bengal a carpet of silk-white sand,
for the hill country streams, a carpet of green,
where the singing fish lulls the full moon,
to gaze on itself and sleep,
in the Batticaloa lake
an expanse of water.
Those from afar, now enjoy all;
those from here, have only grief.

From time immemorial
Ganapathy and brother Mohammad,
sing their songs for the cows to return;
where grass touches the udder
the cow thinks of the calf
the dripping milk
makes a pattern on the earth.

In Spring when flowers abound
in the plains the dance begins,
in the circular arena,
the eyes of the young ones dance.
the breeze pulls away her cloth,
the steps falter, the beat remains steady.

The prince on his steed
goes into battle
vanquishing foes.

Surrounding the prince
heads held high
the soldiers rejoice;
to the annavi's beat
all these in the arena;
on the steps of homes,
unbearably hungry,
they wait
to clasp these hands.

In the landlord's mansion
the harvest done
the songs abound
and hunger is forgotten.
I walk across the city.

The fields and the sea
all wealth now taken as bounty,
in the plains
Ganapathy and brother Mohammed
now lie in conflict?
What can I say?

TO GRANDMOTHER

Hands of the palm trees
framing the waves
perennial as you
my grandmother.

Demons possessing
you relentlessly
have all now fled.

On the ashes of the Portuguese
rise the coconut trees,
fruits for us to pick
from the coconut trees.

On the graves of those
victors by chance
defying time,
my grandmother lives.

Again on your shores
have they appeared,

the vanquished Portuguese?
Speak not of their skin
the colour of their eyes,
they are the Portuguese.

They shall not remain,
a consoling thought;
we will prevail.
The Portuguese will die
the palm trees will grow,
a consoling thought.

Grandmother
in my youth
I danced and sang and romped
and pined,
a life that tortoise-like
along your shores I hid;
the moon that joined in stealth
to pick those fruits
the sun that joined to splash
in rain-fed pools
all these I leave
for those I love.

Rudderless, anchorless,
a sailor adrift
on rafts
I dream of your shores.

A consoling thought
is all that I possess,
you will triumph.

TO A CHILDHOOD SINHALESE FRIEND

Twenty-five years seem like a day,
the past feels like yesterday;
on the mountain slopes of Matugama,
we were butterflies in the Spring;
gold fish swimming in the lake,
monkeys leaping across rubber trees,
all these are like yesterday.

My childhood Sinhalese friend,
even as I meet with you
fluttering,
like doves in flight
a thousand thoughts take wing,
heart bubbles up like beer.

While basking
in the joy of friendship,
something pricks the heart.

Those days,
each lovely evening,
my uncle
his hair grey with wisdom,
forsaking playing
badminton with friends,
abandoning joy,
shrunk with shame
pleading with strangers
studying Sinhala,
do you remember?
How many jeered him,
he swallowed his pride
for a loaf of bread.

Eyes misty, you held my hands,
said farewell and railed against
our suffering.

Thank you my friend!
Yes this too, in twenty-five years,
we often heard.
The list grew
of those who cared.

The burdens too increased,
to burn our shackles
finally,
we stepped into the fire.

CHILDREN OF THE SOIL

Midnight descends in the evening,
pelting rain,
they run, walk, and pause;
floods,
empty streets,
heads buried in a tiny umbrella,
we walked.

Shops made helpless
like wet fowls,
on both sides;
thanks for the rain, said one,
we smiled.
The army in their shelters,
like turtles,
withdrew their khaki heads;
we knew that nature
for her children
on the battlefield
will finish half the task.

Those who joined us
the last time it rained
now covered themselves and slept;

we,
in the roaring flood,
using a raindrop,
write the poem of our lives.

Booted,
to London and Paris,
carrying tiles and lamenting
those with means,
became exiles.
where would we,
poor Tamils
seek refuge?
Even if our fate
must be to rot
shed like the skin
of a snake,
there must be some sense
to the death of humans.

This is our land,
we rise to claim;
in the roaring flood,
using a rain drop,
as we walk
we write the poem of our lives.

IF TEARS MUST BE OUR FATE

Sons and daughters of my land
I bow my head

1.
We, your brothers, tormented you,
we took your land,
severing the cord,
we flung you from the earth's womb;

for five years,
in the North and South,
in foreign lands,
like Cain we asked,
"are we our brother's keepers?"
Even then you did not hate us,
did not stand against us,
for you we still are
brothers.

We have sinned,
we have sinned,
in my days, I have not seen,
people more noble
than you,
the Muslims in the North;
I have not seen
more noble kins;
Even after all this
you called me
to sing your song;
what do I sing
my tears my shame,
my people's shame,
the futile words
of poets like me,
what do I sing?

2.
In the northern shores,
where the ocean breeze,
dries the wet hair,
the tears from your grief,
remain wet;
our land,
like Ahalikai, a stone,
will not rise
until you tread;
the dreams we plucked,

the treasure of your thoughts,
your children's futures,
your tombs
where your ancestors
now wonder,
where your Tamil was lost,
the orchards grown
from their blood and sweat,
the mosques,
where generations,
proclaimed "Allah O Akbar"
all these assembled
we must touch your feet
and seek your pardon,
until then our shackles
will remain.

3.
Five years now
since we sinned;
two years since
sorrow, fault, repentance,
our leaders promised;
Tamils, are you still
asleep?

Having taken all,
under a cruel sun,
along salt dunes,
we chased them away,
the faultless
noble folks;
five years,
they have consumed
rice and tears;
Tamils, are you still
asleep?
Is this the stamp
of your leaders' pledge?

In the sixth year now
if they must weep,
let this land burn,
let my people burn,
let my poetry burn,
let my Tamil burn.

DOMESTICITY

On the river bank,
I am a tree,
undefeated yet.

Today the forest river
moves calmly,
hardly shaking a weed;
squeezing the light, from dawn,
mischievous Holi,
multitude of colours,
it moves with gentle touch.
Yesterday's madness
not mine, it claims.

Until my little ones
sprout into life,
I clutch the dissolving
soil of my roots
to survive in war;
I now forget the despair,
surely,
that was not me.

Yesterday's agony is true;
tomorrow's fear, even more;
but life opens its buds today,
the butterflies flutter their wings,

the fish jump with joy.

This friendship, this life,
a gift for our daily
forgetting.

GOODBYE MOTHER

A visitor
outstaying his welcome,
the midnight sun
shines at home.

Even the call centre women
who come to work
cursing their men
who now sleep
having woken them,
have left;
go away O sun,
leaving me to my sleep
which lover-like,
in the night,
spins eunuch dreams;
take pity on your moon,
who too must
sit at the computer
crying on the internet.

I think of the land
whose mothers
have not slept
for three decades;
when the army moved
she stood by the window
on her feet,
a vigilant goddess;

to light her pyre
the enemy forbade me;
breaking the garrisons
for you a flowered
hearse;
take this from me
the fire of my poems;
farewell.

On graves and mounds,
on the footprints
of my ancestors
who defied the Portuguese,
in the blood spilled
by our youth,
in the palmyrah fields,
flourishing with hope,
in our villages
standing tall with
temples and mosques,
a utopian dream
of our land
we must reclaim.

MY STORY

She is a Bo-tree
a forest in itself,
I am a bird,
measuring the world
with my wings;
when she first saw me
she imagined
a free cloud
under a blue sky.
I imagined her
in the arid land below

a moss-filled pond.

One day
she spread her branches,
gestured to me;
my nest was built there
the next day;
this is how, my friends,
it all started.
Along an arid path
with all our riches
forgetting only water
we began our journey.

She a goddess,
stood straight from the root;
to endure was her life;
for me,
floating on wings,
to pause was death.
She tried,
with her roots
to tie me to the earth;
I tried,
to make her shoot across
the sky with wings,
we both lost.

It is true
I called her lame
in my disdain;
she first looked at me,
called me jetsam,
bird of passage,
a running brook.

Finally in the end,
for house and for kids,
we reconciled;

the truth of a deceptive love,
life's many wiles
we realized late.
Our love in bloom
nothing but a script
once written,
by a life-creating artist.

Now things are clear;
when we meet
I go to my golden Bo-tree.
"I flew across a thousand woods,
but never perched
on any branch but yours."
A delighted Bo-tree says,
"A thousand birds flew
across, but only you
sat on my branches."

This is how, my friends,
a bird and tree
became a tale.

UNKNOWN PASTURES

A grass field,
from my childhood years,
like my yard,
I knew the boundaries;
my heart, its green;
in the far distance,
a small village,
its flagpole the coconut tree;
or a sea dancing and singing
in harmony with the fisherman's song,
or just the horizon.

On these pastures,
where cows graze, shaking their heads,
I wandered the whole day;
At the end in the sky
the sun's paintings on display.
In the east,
in the Gokulam
of our goat herd Krishna
the flute now fell silent.

At dusk when the moon rises,
the wind
together with the expanding darkness
sheds its moisture
as it passes by.

In an evening like this one
I was there;
She too sat there
with a hundred reasons
for not clasping
my hands.

My heart shedding from my eyes,
I burned in your love;
My life spreading on you
you shredded it;
a scorching flame
in a human oyster,
when would I join you
like fire and earth?

I plead
you sat still
like one who would burn
the city of Madurai again?

Showing a scroll
in those days
fate demanded from my heart

a pound of flesh.

She who joined eyes
clasped hands
twinned hearts,
later on a blessed day
merged bodies,
now stood up;
"you will never understand me."
I spat my tears and laughed.

A gold hue at dusk
a glowing field
when the stars
drank the night
it spread out blue,
and white by moonlight.

My pasture,
I knew you
from childhood,
what is your hue,
when does the truth emerge,
in daylight, dusk,
in the light of the moon?

My pride in manhood
my sense of knowing all
would I lose you too?
The woods do not
flower and bear fruit
for the bird
arriving late.

FRAGRANCE

Flying over the Atlantic,
I found her scent;
when we parted,
the birds of Spring
departed;
among the geese
flying south
above the lake,
we hid our tears,
said farewell.
In that Spring
on the shores of the lake
where shoals of salmon
now fertile, swam,
more fragrant,
more in bloom than
any plant,
she sat in my boat.
When she stepped out,
"the fate of Tamils"
she said;
among the lakes of Batticaloa
on the banks
we could have met,
she sighed;
white birds filled the sky.
for one moment
the war ceased,
I heard the drums of dancers,
their songs of joy,
the sounds of anklets;
the full moon and the singing fish
her fragrance in a boat
pierces my heart.

Our children should know
the feasts and rites

we lost;
"let them enjoy,
the Batticaloa lakes"
she said.
"Let the boys win" I said;
"let the girls win" she said;
two worlds
in our entwined hands;
when we parted,
the maples trees lost their green,
the black chipmunks,
sensing the famine,
buried oak nuts in the soil;
the butterflies
reaching for the heavens
in their thoughts,
now everywhere;
trampling and peeling,
the maple leaves,
we get in the car;
like the bus driver,
in front of the hungry
dinosaurs in Scarborough,
she leaves me;
Like a scented
flower among clothes,
in the petals of my thoughts,
the fragrance
of her final embrace
she left for me.

A SUNNY DAY

After many days
the sun on Karl Johan's Gate;
in that South American singer's flute
a new tone of grief.

Always stationary,
like a post box,
still a man,
his posture,
one yesterday,
another today;
his soul
among the admirers
on Karl Johan's Gate,
or in the outskirts of
Machu Picchu.
Where does it roam?

Once upon a time
until the Spaniards came,
their canons thundering,
were these the love songs
his ancestors sang?

When his flute
was a bamboo bush,
did the birds in their nests,
sing these songs?
Who would know?

When the sun shines
on any winter day,
on Karl Johan's Gate
the Norwegians throng;
the eateries and bars
overflow;
coins are flung

for street performers;
like a horse prancing
to chase its flies,
to dispel my longing
I too wander
on Karl Johan's Gate.

AUTUMN THOUGHTS

Summer came and went,
a happy dream;
now the cold in
winged horses
whipping across;
the Northern birds
towards my land
take flight;
like blacks
praying to the sky
an empty oak,
and a solitary magpie
looking at me with disdain.

Magpie, magpie!
all birds now fly
towards my land,
seeking the sun,
why do you remain,
in the cold,
in the North?

As if I would not understand,
the magpie shakes its head;
"I will not understand?"
"How would you know?
Even the Northern birds
seek your land; and you

a traveler,
shook off the dust on your back,
and came here."
The magpie's birds
etched its hot words
in my heart.
"Stay magpie!" I said.

"We understand
your Tamil culture,
did you ever appreciate,
what others have,
the freedom to speak?"
Said the magpie
and flew away.

A vagrant in the sky,
the pathos of a cooled sun.
on earth,
the graying yellow trees,
waving their golden feathers
like a butterfly
a ripe birch leaf
lands on the grass,
like a new refugee.

Everywhere
losing life and claiming comfort,
we are human debris;
Is our land
In perennial autumn,
a lifeless tree?

My son in Jaffna,
my wife in Colombo,
my father in Vanni
my mother in Tamil Nadu,
relatives in Frankfurt,
my sister in France,

me,
a lost camel in Alaska,
in Oslo,
our families,
a pillow's feathers,
flung in the air
by a primate fate?

An orchard
carefully grown
by my ancestors,
I left,
to reach a foreign land.
Who will make an orchard
for my grandson?

Last spring
those lovely girls
their lutes and songs,
their festive stage,
I joined and sang
and broke my heart,
a vagrant.

This is autumn,
a time for nature's despair,
water becomes stone
a long winter.

How long do I endure
my land,
stretched north to south
on the lap of the sea
an emerald veena
strummed by the wind and breeze,
a burden in my heart?
The longing
now a poison in me.

"Don't despair" says
the returning magpie;
"look over there"
It points to the
airport.

GOODBYE

With bag and baggage
I step on the street;
full moon in the sky

lulled by
a chariot
with streamers of stars,
do not cover your face
with the cover of clouds,
bid me goodbye.

On the banks of Coovam,
the prince of slums
even today
plays his flute.
In the tiny thatched huts
the concrete caves
now the dwelling of all.

The city's parched walls
now touched with your
magic wand,
Coovam,
Chennai's winding intestines,
covered with your
silver sheet.

In the concrete jungle
to wait like a wall lizard,

no, not for me.

A thousand birds
a thousand flowers
the breeze
each in its poetry
on this land
with my friends,
in the blood-smelling streets,
to speak to the enemies
in the language they
understand,
let me walk with my gun,
wiping my gun,
let me kiss my lover.

In each yard
surrendering
to the toy gun of a kid
let me lift my hands.

To guard the joys
of our kids,
in my resolve
let me walk.

The city of Chennai
bid me farewell,
the young with their flutes
I must leave.

How do I barter
my freedom
as the cost of exile?

Listen to me,
full moon,
like you,
my heart is filled with light.

Falling,
how would I give my kids
the shackles of oppression?

To those
who now carry toy guns,
our rifles,
we will give tomorrow.
Farewell.

A TRAVELLER`S SONG

Gazing at the CN tower,
I see a solitary wild duck
across the glass windows,
ascending the glittering wind-steps
announcing the Spring,
wiping my tears
with feathers;
the grief of my
mother's death
now melting the snow.

In Toronto's nooks and corners
a stooping Sun
with fingers of light
strokes the streets;
shakes into being
the rainbow,
the glitter of dawn;
all is green,
flowers and butterflies,
nascent colours,
the joy of life.

The world shuddering with birth

me, a lonely raccoon,
roaming the lonely streets;
a new day on the boat with me,
a paradise waited
on the shores of the centre island.
I landed, a solitary Tamil.
To the rest,
someone must announce
that Spring had arrived.

My poor friends,
when I first came,
in Toronto's nooks and corners
there was no life, they said.
To make Scarborough's
teeming houses their own,
three jobs they needed;
this time,
with new-found knowledge of life
they greeted me.
In the 416 area
it doesn't exist, they said.
In the 905 area
it exists, they said,
seeking the third job.
Their mansions
their big cars,
now sigh
empty.

Me, a tourist,
life waylaid me,
everywhere;
the corners of downtown,
the streets now owned
by singers and dancers,
the bars,
on life's pastures,
I milked the wealth

of Spring;
Ontario, a land
surrounded by lakes.

Here too in the front yards,
the flower plants smile;
in my land,
the Spring,
even in the yards of refugees
the hibiscus and beans
flower, shed their scent
on thatched roofs;
Like the grass
with all its jostling.
shoots out its flowers,
finally, life too
must win.

The wings
of the honey bee are mine;
before the leaf-falling
yellow season,
I have distances to travel.

LIFE`S POEM

The snake's eyes in the river bank,
the frog entranced by the flying insect;
a sniffing mongoose, scurrying;
on the deer's green path
a human trap spread out;
that which is fearless
lives;
the Pali river moves on
nourishing some trees,
uprooting others.

Man of Titanic dreams
where in your schemes
lies a floating iceberg?
Yet even in drowning,
you play the violin,
living in death;
condemned to die
a wise Greek man
choosing to live.

Unmarked vehicles roam,
enemy guns open fire,
shackled by murderous friends
waiting endlessly,
the desire to live
flooding over me,
I remain a river of life;
no other poetry in me
but this.

My hands stained only
by the tears of some women;
I hate my bleached poetry
disdaining the human
praising the man;
transcending gender
to reach the human,
that is freedom;
to be rescued by generous
men and women,
that is glorious.

Terrible poetry
I have written at times;
but always I have lived,
a good poem;
ask my Sinhalese friends,
my Muslim brothers and sisters,
when war descended on me,

I tried to be human;
that, then, is my best poem.

To stand straight,
embrace the love of life,
that is my poetry.

Puthuvai Ratnathurai

DECEMBER, A THING OF BEAUTY

The sheet slips
and the piercing cold
prods me awake.
Dawn,
I step outside
to a quiet street;
only a few like me,
a black sari
the asphalt road.
December, a thing of beauty.

I kid you not
if truth be told
December is splendid;
how would he
who sleeps till eight
sense this beauty?
The Nallur bells peal
at half past four;
pervasive beauty;
from my door I watch;
December, a thing of beauty.
"No beginning or end"
songs that wake you.
As each song
ends,
and ends,
the temple bells,
the sound of prayer,
and my wife's beauty
as she wakes me,
her hair and cloth
wrapped together,
all converge;
December, a thing of beauty.

BEAUTY UNSEEN

Bathed in dew the grass sways,
in the distance, the beetle sings,
buds now wink in full bloom,
the breeze now gives a caressing pinch;
the rooster sings from this tree and that,
the breaking dawn all smeared in red;
this prodigious beauty of sunrise,
a land where beauty fades at six.

No deafening sounds at dawn,
a straggler or two on the streets;
the land now cooled opens its eyes
whence the heart that does not melt?
This dawn is for poets;
open your eyes to immanent beauty;
the clouds that gather to hear the music,
dispel as crowds now appear.

The herds to plough jaunt their way,
on the tree, the bird seeks its mate;
the songs that flood the neighbourhood,
the music that melds with song,
heaven created anew at dawn;
daybreak and all these disappear;
eyes that sleep a wasteful thing,
a beauty dispelled at six.

WRITING THE REMNANTS OF A DREAM

A narrow street in a Sinhalese village
dreams of a leisurely stroll
persist after waking up.
Unrealizable dream
stirring old thoughts,
a malicious demon;

my Sinhalese friend's village
where I often rested;
not shunned aside as Tamil
but joyfully accepted;
all that beauty heaped
who created this village?
A piece cut from heaven
who put it here?
No human effort
just a miraculous beauty;
no decorations,
like the well-fed banana tree
a village steeped in beauty.
A constant drizzle
in the mountainside
the clouds moving
a saree drying in the wind;
with an upturned face,
a leisurely flowing river;
in the myriad canals
born as if to bathe
skirts tied chest high
the lotus flowers
bathe unashamed;
east-west across the village
the rail tracks pass.
The tracks and road
stretching side by side;
from trains to buses
and buses to trains
the passengers move across;
a small station
where the express train
does not stop.
You need to cross the river
across the bridge
to reach that.
You must watch the setting sun
from the bridge,

you will desire no more;
the evening
the mountain
the setting sun
the green fields
the gentle wind
the converging lanes
would you dare leave
says the village,
hoarding its beauty.
All that beauty
smiles, and
makes you mad;
a small unpretentious
bus stop.
A few shops,
two schools
for boys and girls.
In the centre
a huge Bo-tree
at its base
a small temple
where Buddha meditates.
Each time as you pass
it tempts you to stay.
To stay and leave,
always a burden for the heart.
like white-clad cotton balls
little girls with flower trays,
going to the temple.
You want to gather them
in your arms
all lovely dolls.
Like the gentle wind,
walking lightly
the young women pass by;
a perennial ripeness
a divine gift for the jakfruit;
thirty years ago,

on a full moon day
I was last there,
in my Sinhalese friend
Chandragiri's home
a final feast for the Tamil friend.
A national fervour
friendship among classes
a worker's revolt that united us,
chatting about this and many others
we meandered in the village,
savouring the chilly air
from the mountains;
if memory serves,
chatting about the foolish old man
who moved mountains.
Chandragiri's sister served us;
when we went to the river
to bathe
and returned
she too joined us.
When we parted
we would meet again
we promised;
to the bus stop
Chandragiri and his sister
walked to say farewell.
All these like yesterday.
Thirty years consumed by time;
why that village in my dreams?
Since then,
I have not met Chandragiri;
where are you now?
In that same house
in the same village?
Having moved twelve times
I now live in Vanni.
Let's forget all that
happened in between.
If you are still a member

of the JVP executive
I curse my present dream;
the chances of our meeting
are now greater.
In that village
on that bridge
across the river
in the fields
caressed by the gentle wind
we can meet.
Tell your sister
I am now a father
of three children.
Let's continue to write
the remnants of a dream;
don't let it slip, as
good friends
good neighbours
caring relatives,
we can live together, now
it is all in your hands.

A POET`S FEARLESS DEATH

If I am not stricken by disease
or felled by enemies,
if I do not perish by these,
I will thrive even in old age;
my poems
will give me the strength of youth.
To walk apace
to swing my arms
bend to pick up a grain of earth;
if I have the strength
I will ascend and fly,
with the courage to face death;
I will love life

as roots with flowers
and flowers with roots, I will live.
With my poems
I will be born again,
alongside those
fighting injustice
I will blossom;
I will not grow old
not be infirm;
my poems will prevent my death.
When the final lines of
my life are written,
do not come close to me;
in the light of a small lamp
a face is all that is needed.
When I was born,
when I was poor
I was alone;
When I give myself to death
I want to be alone;
The sound of Death
ringing in my ears won't agitate me,
I will welcome death;
a mat to lie down
a little water to quench my thirst,
my song in my ears
that is enough,
I will depart.
My body frozen,
when I am a corpse,
do not despair;
when my body lies at home;
sing my songs,
read my poems aloud,
be at peace;
I came
lived
and left;
no, I did my best

and returned;
for me
that will suffice.

AN ELEGY FOR A TEACHER

"Teacher Kandiah" has closed his eyes,
the news reached the marketplace;
everyone was shocked;

he was healthy;
last night,
he stepped outside at midnight
to pee
came back and slept;
in the morning he was found dead;
a good death,
fortunate to die this way;
the news spread across the village,
their courtyard filled with people;
front and back, across the yard,
the village has gathered;
on a bench,
Kandiah lies stretched out;
"aunt Ponnamma"
his wife,
sobbing her heart out,
the house seems to shake;
not a trivial matter, to lose him,
a lynchpin for forty years,
the grief of that loss,
how could she endure?
She is distraught;
a canopy erected in the yard,
two cars left to spread the news,
the coffin,
the stuff for the ritual,

now in the purview of the priest;
betel leaves and cigars are in plenty,
mouths turn red with betel juice;
who is to light the pyre?
Why this question?
Teacher Kandiah was no eunuch,
he fathered seven children;
four boys
three girls;
where are they?
Kandiah's dog sleeps
under the bench;
why this question
about lighting the pyre?
Where are the children?
Aunt Ponnamma keeps sobbing;
the first born in London,
the second in Norway,
the third in Germany,
the youngest in Canada;
one girl in Wattala
the next in France;
that is ok,
where is the last-born Kavitha?
Six months ago,
she left for Switzerland;
who is to light the pyre?
What a shame?
Teacher Kandiah stretched on the bench
aunt Ponnamma continues to wail;
only the teacher's dog,
under the bench,
lies waiting;
a tree without roots,
a walking zombie
he had lived;
the roots he banked on,
severed their source,
in despair he died;

what children,
why live out this lie?
When the eyes cloud over,
there is no help,
why do they need the lids?

THE TEMPLE ACROSS THE FIELD

In our tiny village,
at the further end of the field
that temple.
There is a circuitous
lane for vehicles,
walking single file on the bund
is convenient;
very few devotees wanting boons.
to simply show up and pray
the village has no time;
when the temple bells sound,
from a distance, they
knock on their heads, murmuring
"O Pillayar."
One phrase says it all.
The priest arrives
feeds the god
and leaves;
if you climb the steps
the smell of bat droppings
greets you;
no one to ring the bell;
for the food offering,
two crows
alight on the Nandhi;
the pooja ends,
padlock on the door
the priest hastens to the next temple;
the deity laughs

in the locked sanctum
the focal point of the universe
lies uncared for.
The days pass by, and
the festivals begins;
the village awakens,
the bushes are burnt;
with ochre paint
the outer walls now sparkle.
On a Friday, wearing
a broad-edged vetti, and
a matching shawl, with
cronies on both sides,
the trustee drives up.
A huge gathering in the
outer hall.
The sponsors are given flowers,
the meeting ends on a happy note.
Then,
the flag is hoisted,
a temple without the kodi maram
no way!
The festivities begin;
the main priest
decorates the deity,
now glittering in gold.
Vadai and mothaham are tasty;
the lemon rice garnished,
its smell heavenly;
the priest's wife
a splendid cook;
the village pulls
the chariot;
Night;
the lamps wink;
drums and trumpets
arrive from Inuvil
"tie up the camel"
the songs begin;

the youth
now devour the girls
from the edge of their eyes.
Who is more chaste
Kannaki or Sita?
The debate
continues in the hall.
The kanchipurams,
bursting into laughter,
watch the transgression
of women on stage.
As eyes droop with sleep
the villuppattu begins;
when it ends
it is dawn;
with the money
from archanas,
the pots and pans
from the kitchen,
the priest's family departs.
Again,
the fields become empty,
the scattered bats
return to the halls;

Again in a C-90 scooter
the priest arrives
for a ten-minute pooja;
the deity laughs
in the locked sanctum,
the centre of the universe
lies abandoned.

WAITING

No harm in waiting;
to wait until
my poem's meaning fades
carries no shame.
The perennial burden
to unload
with due respect
is cause for joy.
Suffering,
enduring pain,
this journey to the promised land
now being stopped midway
how painful is that?
The future will scorn us,
but does that matter?
What have we lost?
Even the unloading
was at shoulder-high,
to be resumed again;
a short rest
that is all.
Without sagging legs
to walk spritely
hopeful at heart
intent on the goal
we wait;
no harm in that.
The time to begin,
the strength
renewed every moment
as we rest,
no harm then
no blame,
no shame in waiting.

CRESCENT MOON

How do my fifty years matter?
What else to speak of but the loss of beauty?
Driven by desires and passions,
devoid of stature and lowly;
but "Puthuvai lived, a Tamil poet,
igniting the fires": with these words
of truth and pride, his story ends.

A small dot expanded
became a circle; yet
nothing in my life
to speak of;
that rankles me; nothing but
a rolling stone
ending on the plains;
nothing else to mark
my life.

With nothing to show,
a nobody,
I have moved with the
motion of the river and sky;
those who came to my home
embraced me with their love.
New things I sought,
in these I rejoice.

Not a spider's web,
but clear water; never
bitter, a root constantly
nourishing the tree.
Never known fame;
Like dawn, my life was
pure and soft;
at the agony of others
I wept.

Until now
in my fifty years
drank sparingly;
Have fallen into temptation
not followed it slavishly;
refrained from wrong,
changed my ways;
Ranjith my saviour
enshrined in my heart.

Not even in my thoughts
wished harm to others;
thus have I lived.
This is enough;
now the remaining days
flawless, like a child
I wish to live;
let my days float
free like cotton;
Time, give me this boon.

(Written on December 3, 1998 to mark his 50th birthday)

THOSE DAYS WERE BEAUTIFUL

Those days were beautiful;
they remain young,
those perennial days;
not just those days,
but our thoughts of them;
scrape them away,
a few remnants,
remain to rekindle life.

Those were joyous;
hearts not lined with grief,
days of youth;
dreams of tomorrow in us,

no burden to bear;
no love, no dreams of marriage,
no one needing my money;
food when hungry,
clothes when old ones tear,
money to spend;
for me,
to travel afar
wings on my back;
not a burden to the village,
that a relief for my granny;
reading large books,
for grandpa a source of pride;
were these not enough?
Waxing and waning,
every day got spent;
Five in the evening
friends gather to protest oppression
we chat;
to ingest revolution
Lenin or a Mao Tse Tung;
if neither is available,
there is Fidel
now part of our saliva;
the west side of Nallur temple,
beside where Muthu Vinayagar
now is enclosed,
there was then a library;
across it the broad street,
on its side a carpet of sand;
we seat ourselves,
beside us a "do not spit" bucket
its stench unbearable,
we did not mind;
if we did, we did not show;
a red revolution for the slum dwellers
was all we talked;
from our mouths to the Nallur street,
Mao and Lenin visited frequently;

sometimes Keuneman
and Shan came and went;
at six o'clock,
the temple bell summoned the village;
we got up,
proceeded to the adjoining Vel Vilas;
whoever had money paid,
we ordered tea,
and a vadai to go with it;
maybe a cigarette if possible;
lighting up we return
to where we sat,
and ended at 9 o'clock;
we felt the pangs of hunger,
shedding our revolution by the fence,
we headed home;
that day went by well,
only to begin again the next day;
in Nallai centre those days,
something "free" would happen;
one would sing,
another would play the drum,
sometime a debate,
or a book launch,
nothing really to listen,
but we would watch;
at the end the holy ash,
given as prasad;
we would be annoyed,
we will touch, not wear it;
on occasion,
our group assembles
near the chariot;
as soon as we begin our discourse,
the ochre-clad sadhus leave;
a few beggars,
sidle to listen closely;
the camphor seller laughs;
we cared little about them.

We talked about the revolution;
It was on one such day
that she secured me;
to satisfy my wife,
the lover of then,
I refrained one day from meeting;
later,
I stopped altogether;
yet,
those days were beautiful;
those days were joyous;
those days live forever in me.

YEARNING

Pouring rain in my village,
the lanes flooded;
in knee-high water,
soaked to the skin,
the kids launch their boats.
In the yard,
from the overhanging branch
drops of water.
No one to gather
the hibiscus blooms,
the stem gives way
and flowers drop in the evening;
on the hard ground shapes,
marks of flowing rain water;
to exult, I am no longer there;
another December without me
at home.
The lakes,
Paravai and Pandara
the plains of the our guardian
Pillayar,
covered with water.

Parameswara junction,
its Abirami Vilas dosas
the bonda from Pillayar vilas
in Kondavil,
when will I savour?
To pray when the Nallur bells peal
whence that joy?
On the streets of Jaffna,
when do I roam again?
An empty tree without spring,
a hen
having lost her chickens to predators,
I burn from within;
I will not return
while the devils inhabit the land;
but memories reach for
lost pleasures.
I need my village;
I need my life;
I need again
what I have lost.

THE FROLICKING CLOUDS

Open the eyes
that harbour lightening,
swing your arms,
let the storm begin;
in each step you take,
hear the thunder;
walk; let the times
obey your commands.
Across the skies
corpse-eating vultures;
their spit
causes fire in
settlements below.

In each house
a lament for the dead;
defying these,
with their tiny beaks
the birds collect twigs
to make their nests in trees;
the grazing cows
birthing calves
yield milk;
this is how one lives;
Stand straight,
and let the clouds
ruffle your hair.

RESURGENT DAWN AND A RESTLESS POET

Yesterday too was humid and still;
now my pillow, soaked with sweat
dripping off my neck,
my body sticky, I opened my eyes;
What time would it be?
I wait patiently
for the neighbour's alarm.
A child's plaintive cry in the distance
rose and subsided.
Did the mother's breast fill its mouth?
I walk into the yard;
a quiet moon, behind tangled clouds.
played hide-and-seek.
the bats kept alighting
on my neighbour's spreading
Margosa tree.
Why do they quarrel
for the bitter fruit?
I was annoyed,
what could I do?
In the Mandaitheevu camp,

as if to remind us
that "they" are still awake
a few booming explosions;
that too subsided.
Waking the neighbourhood
and shaking off their sleep
as if to bid farewell,
a vehicle, having drunk
kerosene oil, and
vegetable oil
shattering the beauty
of the night
growls along the neighbouring street;
I am annoyed again;
At the well next door,
the mating sound of rope and pulley;
the Manonmani Amman priest
now preparing to bathe.
Is it 3 o'clock?
No doubt it is 3 a.m.
As always the dogs bark,
and lamp in hand
the Pandaram arrives
denudes the flower trees and leaves.
At four, the gong of Nallur temple bells;
the sound fills the ears,
and all pain disappears
from the heart, the thorns ease out.
I breathe evenly.
Vel Muruga, Vel Muruga
he sings loudly,
as he circles the temple
as if he owns the outer street.
All the wells around
are now a hive of activity;
as the east gathers light
the cacophony of crows.
Where does it disappear,
the calm of the night?

For a fresh dawn tomorrow,
I will wait;
lovelier to long for,
than to experience.

THE SCULPTOR AND THE STATUE

Chisel on rock
the sculptor carves his statue.
Still, the beautiful statue
speaks;
beads on the forehead at dawn,
grasping the anklet, the statue opens its eyes.
The sculptor, squatting,
awaiting his betel leaves
hears the voice;
a majestic voice,
a familiar metallic voice;
the sculptor turned to look
the statue spoke:
Listen,
said the authoritative voice
what travesty is this?
Large breasts
narrow hips,
huge navel,
elephant like buttocks,
head resting on shoulder
posture of combing its hair;
how long would this last?
In Rajarajan's female quarters
in Mahendra Varman's protected hall,
all your ancestors
embellished the breasts.
Swear to me
weren't you torn
carving out those vessels of joy?

Were those breast divine?
A statue of a beggar,
of a firewood seller
a child fallen in battle
did your hands create?
A sea of tears
the fire of hunger
the pain of struggle,
are these so harsh
that you cling to my breasts?
Today I knew
why I sweated
each time you touched me.
At your touch
I come to life;
but no,
let me like Akalikai
remain inert.
But you don't
touch me.

MOVING RIVER

Carrying us on its ripples,
our life still lit despite the wind
travelling this distance
a tormented river;
from a benighted spot
shedding incessant tears
its journey grew;
thorny shrubs along its way
it walked, panting.
tongue parched and weary
it moved;
smashed against blocking trees
it lifted its arms and wailed;
save the flame from dying

screamed the ripples;
unshaken in its faith
of a brightening day
the river moves.
One multiplies into ten
the river swells and grows.
Now the deception
of a verdant shore;
the river must not stray
beguiled by beauty;
even poisonous flowers are fragrant;
the heart aches to pluck them;
new dams are built
to divert the river;
the beguiling koels
sing on the banks;
until the sea is reached
the river must remain unruffled;
bursting the dams,
let the river move.

SILENCED, THE TEMPLE BELLS

What kind of imprisonment?
Like Sita in the forest
how long amidst the demons?
Pleasing the devils with a smile,
feathers clipped
life in the cage;
fearful during the day.
a few cautious steps,
in the night
ears against the door
waiting;
the sound of stamping boots
the new music;
freezing when the dog barks,

rendered speechless,
what kind of torment?
The temple bells now mute,
the nathaswaram sheathed at four,
the festivals conclude
within the walls,
the midnight pooja in the evening;
the gods turn a blind eye,
why should they bother?
Until the door opens next day
the god does not stir abroad;
in the morning,
one dove leaves for work
the thali pressed to the eyes
the other dove bids farewell;
what certainty
to be sure of returning
in the evening?
A tenuous life;
at the school gates
the old folks wait
to take their grandchildren home;
the next funeral,
who knows when.
Let them mock
it doesn't matter.
Until now
in the fenced yards,
the restricted life had its joys.
Empty rituals
jaded relations,
but life was majestic.
Funerals,
rituals
memorials
anniversaries
even the grief is communal,
a fullness of life.
All slipped away;

a worm tormented in the sun
the pain now routine.
Those days
in the night, however late
after the Sinnamman temple festival
one could return home;
no street lights
no fear either;
today,
terrified
not only on the street,
but even at home;
the fear of
a knock on the door
sleepless,
we spend our days.

THE POET, THE WIND, AND THE FLOWERS

Until yesterday, the sky looked beautiful;
then someone struck a match,
the clouds began to burn;
the moon too was trapped;
the wind that blew the clouds,
escaped,
letting the clouds burn;
no one to douse with water,
the entire sky is ablaze;
the poet watching from below
was furious;
he summoned his words,
looked up in anger
and wrote his poems;
then he went to sleep;
the escaped wind,
did not idle;
from snowy lands,

for the clouds
for the sky,
it organized
memorials;
now the stars,
began to douse the fire;
they burned and died;
they flowered and burned
to douse the fire;
the wind and the poet
offered their poems,
now sleep again;
the advancing stars
will save the clouds.

ON THE THIRD DAY AFTER THE FESTIVAL

The bustle,
the sounds of prayer
the hailing vendors
all subside;
Velevan street now lies empty;
the crowded Nallur streets
now pleasant again.
The peanut foils
swirl in the wind
and settle;
the empty streets are
beautiful.
"Spit Here" buckets
not removed as yet;
the emptiness
devoid of human presence,
still lovely.
Will no one come to me,
yearn the chariot steps;
tired from all the activity

Valli now asleep;
Theivanai anxious
at not seeing her father
has gone back to the heavens.
Murugan still playful
astride his peacock
left in the morning,
has not returned;
the temple door locked,
the antenna on the priest's house
now being adjusted
for Pothihai.
The Muttu Vinayagar on West street
the Manonmanin Amman in the corner
desolate,
who will now visit them?
The acrobats performing
in the constructed well,
removing the planks
have left for the Vallipuram temple.
Where would the snake charmer
have gone?
Festival is now festivity.
All have chosen silence, and
focus on the revenue;
the orators,
now with their gold shawls
are satisfied.
The sacred thread
across his chest
a Brahmin made Rotti
he is a radical;
that deserves our tribute.
What is earned stays with you;
this is greater than temple service;
Where the Thileepan memorial stood,
even among the defaced stones,
were any flowers placed?
Forget those who destroyed,

how about those
who sat on the rubble?
This time too
the festival was a success
an old-timer said in passing;
I was amused.

FULFILMENT

Among the coconut trees
a breeze frolics; night insects
flaunts their music; listening,
the Margosa tree nods its head,
the young bull chews the cud;
my old ones panic; wondering,
"has he come?" "will he?"
Lie stricken at the door.
The streets deserted,
the moon sheds its light
with no one to watch.
My village
stretching beyond Neerveli
now sleeps; the folks that
cradled and rocked me to sleep,
now starve and wait for me.
Harness your chariot, Sun,
spread your light
dispel the darkness.

The streets where I walked;
the womb that carried me,
now in the hands
of armed demons;
having left, I roam;
dog-like I live;
I need to return,
I need the Nallur temple,

the long night must end;
give me the grace
to return home,
to stand up straight.

GRANT ME A WISH

The mountain
a breast for the clouds to caress
On the dew-filled grass
the sun glitters;
at my feet;
a warbling stream flows.
As it strokes
the nubile trees
its moist lips brush past me
on its way to heaven.
Here is a beauty
denied to my village.
"A thousand eyes will not suffice"
a poet here
might have written.
Had this beauty been mine as well,
how much would I have written?
Burnt to ashes
that poem
died.
At my life's end
I yearned
to live and die here;.
the villains
stoned my dreams.
I see this again,
that alone is enough.
Now in my village shrubs,
in the shadow of the
Ilanthai tree,

let me lie
and end my life;
grant me this wish.
Yesterday my great grandfather,
then my grandfather
tomorrow my father,
in the cemetery where they burned,
I too must burn.
God, will you grant me this wish?

THREE QUESTIONS

Time for peach fuzz

A large moustache for the old man
like a machete;
for the boy peach fuzz,
like moss.

A fowl on the front steps;
peach fuzz throws a stone
"kill" says the machete.

A dog visited the yard;
the boy watched,
"smack it" said the old man.

Circling the village
spreading thorns
the pride of ownership
the horned bulls
walk through the fence.

The boy picks up a stone,
"fool, put it down"
the old man panicked.

"Why?" says peach fuzz aloud.

"These bulls will pierce and kill,
lie low and survive,"
whispers the machete.

"Bows to the mighty
attacks the weak,"
murmurs peach fuzz,
looking at the machete.

RELATIONSHIP

As my writing persisted
so my poetry grew;
lines stretched into form
the poem now beautifully shaped,
I sat it on my lap
combed its hair;
why did you create me
asked the poem.
Each day that I create
my life becomes a blessing.
My poem smiled and spoke:
with words you created me,
a beautiful canvas,
your art now perfected.
the nerves now alive
the lungs have breath
you are my father
a Brahma by creating me,
said the poem.
I floated in joy.
Yet a slight misgiving
the soul insisted I speak,
I spoke:
You are a sculpture
chiselled by me,

I did not create you
for yourself
but for me!
When my heart catches fire
you open your eyes.
Not for you did I create
but for myself.
Laughingly it kissed me
and departed,
my poem.

BEAUTY AND THE SEA

Like fingers pinching the lover's waist,
waves caressing the shore,
lightly nibbled the land;
the tiny waves,
the spittle from its kiss,
spread across the shore;
the ocean's water
seeping across Vattuvahal
now becomes Nadhi Kadal.
The beauty of this stream!
In the spell of the night,
this sea becomes heavenly;
in the light of the moon,
beauty's reign in the sea;
counting the stars,
watching with yearning,
the night birds flying across,
sitting on the shore is bliss;
when I went there was none
just me alone,
all this beauty for one.
Today, surprisingly,
net in hand, another,
surprised to see me;

who are you, he asked,
moving closer;
I was startled, he laughed;
what beauty in the sea, I said;
he seemed bemused;
is this the time for beauty,
his look implied;
I catch crabs,
sometimes prawns,
in the morning I wash my back,
where is the beauty in this?
he walked into the sea,
I stood up to return;
no thoughts of beauty,
he, with his net, in the sea;
this sea, his daughter,
for me, my lover;
same woman, different ties;
I walked away.

BRIGHT EVEN IN THE NIGHT

The hot sun scorches the body.
Is it noon, already?
Is it dark only at night?
Now even the days are dark;
what would I do at home?
Outside, hardly anything to do;
today like yesterday,
tomorrow like today,
the days pass by,
unchanging;
me helpless,
my wife needing care,
the five-year old
knows nothing;
simply laughs and cries;

rented land,
rented house,
rented rice,
the deep roots severed,
my life in shambles;
Yaman entered our city
to redeem us;
the neighbouring country
now here for peace;
a war for peace, say,
the Sinhalese state;
only our backs,
bear the burden;
what fate is this?
Let history tell
that they returned,
because we chased them;
a squirrel carrying earth,
to the dam,
a Tamil true to my conscience,
duty-bound, a man of the time,
let me live;
who says that days are dark?
That was yesterday;
today it shines at night.

OUR FOLKS ARE NOT UNGRATEFUL

The Nallur festival has ended,
even the wind has departed,
leaving the temple street desolate;
twenty-five days of joy,
still fresh in the heart,
with longing eyes, some youth
still wander to see the chariot;
only those who have seen,
would know the pangs
of missing those sparkling eyes;

the different chariots,
now all inside;
the chariot enclosed,
its golden tip hidden
until next year;
the Navalar hall padlocked;
on West street
Muthu Vinayagar remains silent,
a single wick burns inside;
at the entrance
of Manonmani temple,
a few stragglers, me
and some dogs;
from where did the crowds gather?
like an empty sea,
where did they disappear?
The crowds on temple street
are beautiful;
thousands around me,
proclaiming,
I am not alone,
a source of joy.
Without seeing the chariot,
the marriage of the gods,
who stood guard at the gates?
while the silk-dressed anklets
came here,
who stood awaiting the enemies?
Like saints free of desire
who stood there to protect?
Those who came to the festival
their possessions locked.
their keys intact, to
whom did they entrust their land?
Unwashed faces and dishevelled hair
these border gods with guns
stood guard;
with scythes stood some others;
Did the silk dresses at the festival,

pray for them too?
Sure they did,
our folks are not ungrateful.

WHERE SNOW FALLS

Friend,
forgive me;
for this tardy reply;
I was away in Vanni;
when I returned,
your letter was on my desk,
and now my reply.
In your troubled words,
in the stain of your tears,
my heart melted.
Your body in a land of snow,
your mind still dwells
on the mango tree
in the yard.
I am pleased with
the migrating bird's
impulse to return.
If only this,
I am content.
The memory of your mother's lap
remains intact.
Do not grieve,
times will change
you will return
from your journey.
In that alien land
among alien faces,
who will miss you?
In the frenzy of mornings,
who will notice you?
A dead leaf

on the edge of a river
is no consolation;
what can you do but
change with the times?
The gabled roofs of the street,
the temple festival
of the tin-roof Ganesh,
peanut vendors,
bangle shops,
the drummers on West Street,
do not dredge up these thoughts;
remembering the past is painful.
Learn to grow roots
in the new soil.
You asked for our news;
as always
events came and went;
the school prize function,
the library's annual party
all took place;
Varathalinga appu's niece
brother Selvarajah's son,
"they have gone
where they must".
You will understand; and
the music concert
the young artists,
the Saddanathar temple festival
all took place,
lovely beyond compare.
Vasudeva Nanayakkara came and left.
A procession two days ago
to remove the blockades;
I too joined,
you could have been here
it was a mistake to leave.
I see your Puvanam often,
a gentle smile
and she disappears:
poor thing.

Nagalingam's house
—he left for Germany—
is now a camp for the 'boys.'
Tall metal fences,
nothing can be seen;
they come and go;
sometimes the lamps are lit.
"We seek the enemy's barracks"
this song we often hear.
Asking for curry leaves one day,
a small "boy" came home,
dressed in civil clothes.
"What are you cooking today?"
I asked.
"Meat and gravy"
he replied.
"Which village are you from?"
He chose not to reply.
"What is your name?"
"Periannan" he said.
"How many battles have you fought"
I asked in jest
"Including Punagari, seven" he said.
I was stunned.
Full grown courage now
waits to be harvested;
this soil is unlike any;
To have lived here
during these times
that alone is enough.
You
must learn to assimilate
or must return.
All are well,
will write
when you do,
forgive the delay,
my friend.